ENDORSEMENTS

There are moments in life that God has uniquely and especially prepared for us. I have had the experience of living life with Rev. Samuel Stephens for the last 25 years. I have witnessed him stepping into *kairos* moments. God has been faithful to honor his obedience. This book is not written from theory but from the living experience of following God in obedience and seeing what He can do when an individual prepares to live in the *kairos* moments.

—DR. CLAUDE ROBOLD, Pastor Emeritus, New Covenant Church of God (Middletown, Ohio)

It sounds a bit strange, but I had a *kairos* moment as I read *The Kairos Moment*. Set in India, it nonetheless will impact readers anywhere with its solid biblical principles of leadership in the Kingdom. For me, the *kairos* moment came in the powerful ways the author spoke of balancing strategy and organization with being Spirit-led. Whether it is India or Indiana, I needed that and you will too.

—DAVE BUTTS, President, Harvest Prayer Ministries

Church history reveals a startling fact—the kingdom of Christ does not simply advance incrementally, but also in dramatic surges marked by the extraordinary work of the Holy Spirit. Our brothers and sisters in the India Gospel League are catching such a wind from heaven right now.

Their story inspires and guides. Thanks be to God: today is the day of salvation!

—**DEL FEHSENFELD,** Senior Editor, Revive Magazine, Life Action Ministries

Samuel Stephens' vision to ask pastors to start a new work in an unreached village every year is producing tremendously for the Kingdom of God. India Gospel League is now reaching millions with the gospel and their goals are ever-increasing, as they lean into *kairos* moments in service to the Lord. This book holds a tremendous message for all of us in strengthening our relationship to Christ. We too can find our *kairos* moments as we leave behind traditional ways of doing ministry in order to follow the Lord's special instructions.

—**DONNA THOMAS,** Project Partner & Christian Vision Ministries

Through his leadership of India Gospel League, Sam Stephens has become one of the most prolific Kingdom builders of our generation. What he provides in *The Kairos Moment* is a window into how he sees God's Spirit moving mightily among the least and lost in South Asia, in a magnitude we can barely comprehend. You will be greatly inspired by this incredible account. Come along for the journey!

—**JOHN DREYER,** President of The Shelby Group, Chicago, IL & Volunteer for India Gospel League's North American Team

Sam Stephens is among the best strategists and practitioners of Kingdom work I've ever encountered. God has His hand on him in a mighty way. *The Kairos Moment* lets us in on some of Sam's thinking. We need to listen to him!

—REGGIE MCNEAL, Missional Leadership Specialist, Leadership Network and author of *Kingdom Come*

With clarity and conviction, Sam Stephens shares how the gospel is spreading in rural villages by Third Wave church planters. These indigenous believers, in concert with the Holy Spirit's power and guidance, are planting thousands of churches and bringing social transformation to thousands of villages, and, I might add, doing so with few resources. Denominations, mission organizations, missionaries—the usual vehicles of cross-cultural church planting and social change—are being passed by for a fresh explosion of the Spirit's movement among the people who live their lives in rural areas. I challenge you to read this book for three reasons. First, to celebrate how the Gospel is bringing about abundant spiritual and social change in South Asia. Second, to consider if God is calling you to partner with India Gospel League. And third, to learn the principles for seeing God's *kairos* moments in your place of ministry. This story, this book, will inspire you as it has truly inspired me.

—DR. MARYKATE MORSE, George Fox University & Seminary

A *kairos* moment is something we all desire but can so easily look past in our ambitious human approach Kingdom work. As Sam suggests, our goal should be to be in tune with and unstructured enough to allow the Holy Spirit to truly lead, yet organized enough to operate well! It's amazing how biblical principles transcend cultures, demographics and affluence. A very challenging book!

—**PETER DAVIS,** Leadership Team, Life Action Ministries, Canada

I have known Sam for a number of years and I'm proud that our church has enjoyed a long-term partnership with India Gospel League to impact that region of the world with the love and message of Jesus Christ. I can confidently say that Sam is a ministry multiplier who doesn't just talk about ministry; he really mobilizes people to get things done. As a result, he is a fruit-bearing leader of wisdom. I truly believe *The Kairos Moment* will inspire you to grasp hands with Sam and his team so we can fulfill the Great Commission together.

—**TOM MULLINS,** Founding Pastor, Christ Fellowship (Florida)

If you've ever thought, "There must be a better way to do missions!" then you need to read Sam Stephens' new book. With decades of field experience, Sam has the credibility and humility to challenge our thinking in this critical area. I highly recommend this book to pastors, ministry leaders, and those engaged in mission endeavors around the world.

—**TIM NEPTUNE,** CEO of Leadership Outreach and Pastor of Venture Church (Naples, FL)

"Is now the opportune time?" is the second most important question you can ask. I believe every believer in Jesus across the world should ask two questions, "What is God's will for my life, and is now the time to go after it?" Pastor Sam brilliantly answers the latter in his new book *The Kairos Moment*. Sam does an incredible job of showing us how to identify those big moments in life, and then offers great tools for stepping boldly onto that path. This book is a must-read for pastors, ministry leaders, volunteers, and everyday believers who have a burden on their hearts and are trying to decide if now is the time to move."

—**JOSH MAUNEY,** Director of Church Planting, USA Association of Related Churches (ARC)

In *Kairos* Samuel Stephens shares a vision for the spread of the gospel in India; but it was not originally *his* vision. Rather, he discerned what the Holy Spirit was already doing and aligned the priorities and strategies of India Gospel League accordingly. The results were exponentially more than he could have expected from following the typical route to a larger organization. Rev. Stephens' words will hit hard in the West, where so often the church's efforts are spent on growing structures, institutions, and individual congregations. You will be challenged, you will be encouraged, and you are invited to see new opportunities.

—**JOEL W. HUGHES** Ph.D., Elder, Xenos Christian Fellowship of Northeast Ohio

THE KAIROS MOMENT

IS NOW THE OPPORTUNE TIME?

SAMUEL STEPHENS

PUBLISHED BY

United States of America

THE KAIROS MOMENT

Printed in the United States of America.

Published by India Gospel League, North America
www.IGLWorld.org

Editorial assistance: Dan Jarvis of Life Action Ministries
and India Gospel League - North America, Karen Roberts
of RQuest, LLC, and the whole team at the India Gospel
League - North America office in Hudson, Ohio.

Design: Liza Hartman and Tom Jones

ISBN 978-1-934718-59-9

DEDICATION

To the two most important women in my life: my mother, Sarojini Stephens, and my wife, Pratibha.

TABLE OF CONTENTS

FORWARD

The air was heavy, burdened by the humidity and scent of burning dried dung, scrap wood, and agricultural waste. The press of humanity that greeted me outside of the Bombay Airport (yes, in those days the city was still named Bombay – today, Mumbai) literally took my breath away. Five thousand, at least, would be my guess: local Indians pressed against each other in the middle of the night, hawking rides into the city, vying for the attention of travelers managing too much luggage, staring at the dazed passengers disembarking from their overnight flight from Frankfurt. These masses had not come to greet me, of course, but one of their number did; his name was Samuel Stephens. It was October, 1987, Rajiv Gandhi was the Prime Minister of India, the Cold War was still in play, Hong Kong remained a British Crown Colony, and American heartthrob Zac Efron was born.

Samuel Stephens was in 1987 as he is today, a man of singular vision. An Indian patriot whose deep love for his country and people is exceeded only by his devotion to the cause of their redemption and the realization of their promise. I landed in India that dark night not certain what to expect. I had traveled widely abroad before—in the developed world, Europe mostly—but never to what we used to brand as the Third World, those nations on the globe caught between the First (western, wealthy) World and the Second (less affluent, but still influential, actors on the stage of current events, led by the Soviet Union). Officially non-aligned (with either of the global superpowers), India nevertheless seemed to lean toward Moscow. Famed for its exotic images (think: Taj Mahal, tigers and elephants, elaborate Hindu temples) and pitied for its poverty (think: starving children and materially desperate village scenes), India was a complex mystery, hidden behind a veil of my own ignorance and the black and white newsreels from an age long gone.

Cows. Curry. Crowds. These I knew would be a part of the weave. But, I was wholly unprepared for what would next unfold, over a three-week journey, that I can safely say forever changed the course of my own life.

I had been invited to speak to several hundred Christian pastors in the south of India, during a five-day convention. This opportunity had been passed on to me by Donna Thomas, an American missionary-entrepreneur, with whom I was not previously acquainted, but who had heard of me. She asked if I would accompany her to the church conference—and then travel about the country with a young man she did not know either, but who had invited her to see the ministry he led; his name was Samuel Stephens.

Donna was old enough to be my mother; India was not a destination of which I had ever dreamed; traipsing about the subcontinent for weeks with her and another man neither of us knew was highly improbable—preposterous, really. Still, for some reason I can only interpret as Divine, I agreed to go.

Samuel Stephens stood with a sign at the Bombay airport, in the chaos of waving arms and broken English, mixed with the Marathi language the city calls its own. It read simply, "Donna Thomas and Friend." We made our way through the crowd, which implausibly included several cows and wild pigs, threw our bags into a cab with our host and sped off to catch some sleep in a 10th floor guest house, held for vagabonds like us. Finding my way in the dark of the room to which I had been assigned, at 3:00 a.m., slipping off my sweat-drench shirt and cargo pants to climb into bed, I was startled to find another young man stretched out on the mattress. "What's up, mate?" he said quizzically, as I practically tumbled on top of him. He was a New Zealander, hitching-hiking around the world, in the guest house for a day. My adventure had hardly begun.

Over the next few weeks, Samuel Stephens would introduce me to his world. It was not just the spectacular world of India—a nation so diverse, so rich in its tapestry of tradition, art, and history as to defy volumes of storytelling—but also to his world of dreams and godly ambition. From day one, it was clear that Sam loved India, but also believed it could be so much more. This thirst for more life, more hope, and more and better days for his country was altogether consequent to his deep faith in Christ. Sam was—and is—a man who believes that the future success and peace of India is hinged on its growing openness to embracing the Gospel which has transformed so many other nations before.

After a rewarding few days working with pastors in Kerala, Sam took Donna and me (by train, by car, by elephant, by plane) across the vast subcontinent. From Cochin (Kochi) to Calcutta (Kolkata), from Madras (Chennai) to Agra, from Hyderabad to Aurangabad, from Jaiphur to Delhi, and so many places in between, we crisscrossed territories once governed by Muslim Mogul emperors, Hindu maharajahs, Buddhist potentates, the Viceroy of the Raj, in the footsteps of the Mahatma, Gandhi himself, and along the road to independence which, in the late 1940's gave birth to this, the world's largest democracy.

More significantly, Sam walked with us where Jesus walks: in the impoverished rural countryside, into the teeming town markets, alongside lepers, into villages where the blind were made to see and the lame made to walk, literally, by the proclamation of the same Good News that turned the Roman Empire upside down so many centuries before. The dynamic, New Testament-like, Holy Spirit engineered advance of the Lord's healing and redeeming touch was palpable.

And, as we traveled, I watched Sam. I watched him believe in the power of God to claim a nation. I watched Sam reach by faith beyond what could be imagined or known by human reason. I watched him—and the ministry team of the India Gospel League with which he works—dare to do what no one thought possible.

Sam's passion does not foresee the submission of India to western culture or values; indeed, he is a proud defender of the strong fabric of Indian culture, family systems, and diverse histories, at every point they bring life. But, he knows that what we believe about God, how we understand He Who made us, is key to releasing the power of all that is good in this world, and in India. He knows that Jesus is the face of God, the Word become flesh, and that in His life, death, and resurrection, a better world today—and for tomorrow—can be found. This is true for all nations, all peoples, and, yes, India, as well.

In 1987, I thought Sam's aspirations noble, but a distance beyond my ability to grasp. I, too, believe in the Gospel and have seen my own life turned for the good by embracing Christ as Lord. But, the whole nation of India? Seriously? A nation steeped in Hindu gods, a nation with 900 million Hindus, a nation with the second largest Islamic population on earth, the nation in which the Buddha was born and launched his thousand ships into the sea of competing religions? Can India, so long a pawn of western empire and mercantile imperialism, ever divorce its understanding of Jesus from the long shadow of the Raj and worse? The whole proposition, though well-intentioned, seemed beyond the pale.

But, that was then, and this is now. In the over quarter century since my first visit, I have been an eyewitness to the transformation of tens of thousands of Indian communities by the Gospel's power. I have seen whole swaths of the country move from, as Jesus promised Paul (Acts 26), "the kingdom of darkness into the kingdom of light." I have been persuaded that, yes indeed, the advance of the living Jesus across India in these days can, in fact, change the face of the nation.

Much must still be done. These dreams are not fanciful, but they do take time. And resources. And partnerships. And prayer. And commitment. Still, these are things the Lord Himself provides, proved true over the years, often by the hands and life-altering investments of people like you and me.

Rajiv Gandhi's mother, Indira, was murdered as Prime Minister two years before I first visited Bombay; Rajiv succeeded her. He would be murdered four years after my first visit. Their Congress Party which so long dominated the Indian political landscape, has ebbed and flowed. The Soviet Union is no more and the non-aligned community of nations, of which India was once at the helm, has, also passed away. Hong Kong is now a possession of the People's Republic of China. Zac Efron still warrants an autograph here and there, but may not hold legions of teens in his palm as he once did, any more.

And, India? Cows. Curry. Crowds. They're still there, in abundance. And Sam Stephens? He is still at work, hardly even approaching his prime, changing India, for Heaven's sake. The window is open; it is a *kairos* moment, perhaps, a time like no other. This book tells the tale. Walk into its pages and maybe, just maybe, you'll discover what I long ago learned: God is at work in India. He can be at work in your land, too. Never underestimate Him.

—**Jim Lyon** General Director, Church of God Ministries
(Anderson, Indiana)

CHAPTER 1

LIFT UP YOUR EYES

T here are moments, divine moments, that God uses to shape history.

Pentecost. The burning bush. The courage of Daniel in the midst of lions. The dreaming of young Joseph. The coming of Christ.

I like to call these moments "*kairos*" (a concept we will more fully explore throughout this book). In short, this ancient Greek word signifies the "opportune time"—*a special moment when something miraculous happens, when everything is ready, when the foundations have been laid, when decisive action must be taken, when God's prevailing purpose becomes clear.*

Think back to a *kairos* moment in your own life, perhaps the day you learned of Jesus for the first time or the day you sensed His call upon you. You might also recognize these moments in the life of your family or in your church community. Times of spiritual breakthrough. Times of great and unexpected change.

In my country, India, I believe we are experiencing a nation-wide *kairos* moment, an opportune time when the Holy

Spirit is touching lives and transforming communities in ways that, a few generations ago, no one would have anticipated. In some cases, it is happening in ways that no one would have even believed feasible. But God's power is at work. Something special is happening, unprecedented in the history of my culture. A divine moment is most certainly upon us.

The chapters ahead will reveal how God's work that is taking place across my nation is advancing dramatically. They will also lay out a scriptural pattern for how people like you and I can recognize and respond to a *kairos* moment.

FOUR MONTHS MORE?

On his way to Galilee, Christ stopped to rest near a Samaritan well and struck up a rather culturally inappropriate conversation with a woman who was there to draw water. After speaking with her about spiritual ("living") water, Jesus let her in on the truth few people had yet grasped: He was, indeed, the promised Messiah. But the story does not end there.

Before this encounter, Jesus' hungry disciples had ventured off to purchase food. Upon their return to the well, they were shocked to find the Savior in the midst of a theological conversation with a woman. Rather than question Jesus along these lines, they began encouraging Him to eat, blatantly missing the incredible gospel opportunity in front of them.

The disciples did not see the open heart of this woman, and they were not looking for it. Had this particular journey been up to them instead of their rabbi, they would have taken another route altogether, never encountering this particular community. After all, Jews and Samaritans rarely interacted with one another.

But Jesus knew this was a special encounter, a *kairos* moment for the city of Sychar. He said to His confused disciples, "My food is to do the will of him who sent me to accomplish his work. Do you not say, 'There are yet four months, then comes the harvest'? Look, I tell you, lift up your eyes, and see that the fields are white for harvest" (John 4:35).

Soon the entire village had surrounded Jesus on the basis of this woman's testimony, and within a few days many became believers. They said to the woman, "It is no longer because of what you said that we believe, for we have heard for ourselves, and we know that this is indeed the Savior of the world" (John 4:42).

The disciples weren't intentionally trying to miss a cue from the Holy Spirit that this woman's community was a field "white for harvest." But then again, they had no expectation of God's work there either. To them this chance encounter was part of a routine stop for water and food in the midst of their busy ministry journey. Without seeing it, they had stepped directly into a *kairos* moment. The fields were ready for harvest. They needed to lift up their eyes, Jesus said, to see the larger work God was doing around them.

- *What if you encounter such a moment, at such a place?* Will your eyes be open to purposes beyond your own, prayerfully considering what God might be doing outside of your paradigm, your planning, your church, or your methodology?

- *What if God does something unexpected among "Samaritans" in your culture?* I'm quite sure the disciples had never thought of that possibility, so it caught them off guard. Additionally, their cultural biases made it difficult for them to imagine God working in ways outside of their own expectations.

- *What if God uses means that are culturally unconventional to you?* I can't imagine that Peter, John, and James were expecting a spiritual awakening to begin with an immoral woman in a Samaritan village.

- *What if God asks you to go to place far outside your own comfort zone?* These road-weary travelers probably couldn't wait to get back to familiar Jewish territory.

I hope the disciples' response, at least initially, doesn't describe what yours and mine could be in a *kairos* moment. But I think it could. It is very possible for us to get so used to "our way" of doing ministry, "our way" of seeing God working, "our way" of church organization, and "our way" of schedules and budgets and volunteers that we miss the harvest all around us!

I've seen this tendency in India, particularly when it comes to mission efforts intended to reach the more than 350,000 unreached communities remaining in the nation (as of 2016). I've seen churches and even whole denominations enter India, intent on doing evangelization or compassionate work among the poor, seemingly stuck in traditional patterns of the past or methodologies "proven" in other parts of the world. Sometimes these efforts are so off the mark that they do unintentional harm to the advance of God's kingdom.

Have you seen a similar tendency in your culture?

One reason it happens is because, rather than seeking God for a *kairos* moment, people try to create their own. Or perhaps worse, they try and duplicate work God has blessed elsewhere, assuming the same conditions exist everywhere. To avoid this mistake, it is important that all of us ask not only, "What has God done?" but also, "What is God doing now, and what is He doing *here*?"

SOMETHING SPECIAL IS HAPPENING, UNPRECEDENTED IN THE HISTORY OF MY CULTURE. A DIVINE MOMENT IS MOST CERTAINLY UPON US.

I too was involved once in a form of ministry to my people that, in the long run, would have missed the movement of God in our culture. Something new was happening in South Asia, a new opportunity for the gospel's advance, and it challenged not only the traditional construct of missionary activity but me as well. A *kairos* moment had arrived, and it necessitated a major decision for me and for the organization my father had left in my care. India Gospel League needed a redefinition.

There are many stories to tell about this redefinition, and I'll share some of them with you in the chapters ahead. But here, at the beginning, I wish to challenge you to do exactly what Jesus asked His disciples to do in this story in John 4:1-42.

Will you lift up your eyes? Beyond the busyness of your job or household, beyond the responsibilities and ministries you may have in your church, beyond the expectations you've set for your own future, and even beyond what you've previously seen the Lord do, would you pray for God to show you His harvest? His plan?

HOW MANY?

In India today, there are approximately 650,000 village communities, and India Gospel League estimates that more than 350,000 still need their first church.

DISCUSS IT

1. Can you point to a *kairos* moment in your own life? Was it when you first trusted in Christ? What about since then?

2. What factors might cause people to miss a *kairos* moment? In their own life or family? In their church?

3. From your perspective, what are the top two or three ways God has been working in your community or a community close to yours over the past year? Have you been able to join God in this work?

CHAPTER 2

CHANGING DIRECTION

I didn't feel ready. I wasn't expecting things to happen when they did, even though I was being groomed to lead my father's ministry, India Gospel League.

In 1948, my grandfather founded the ministry in Salem District, and he and my father led it forward to serve many people in our family's region of South India. Then it happened—my father's death in April of 1988. It threw me into fear and apprehension. Was I ready to lead? How would I take the organization forward? How would it grow to the next level? At the time, India Gospel League was limited geographically and was a smaller organization than it is today. And we were definitely facing challenges when it came to resources and leadership.

In the fall of 1988, I took a trip to the United States to seek help in establishing and funding the ministry. By God's grace, support started to build up, and I started to think differently about future growth. However, I was still thinking in a traditional way—about *organizational growth*. I had in mind only to start additional ministry projects (such as a Bible school) from which we could train and send out church planters. So I focused all of my effort in that direction.

That's when the *kairos* moment began.

The Lord started bringing to my attention a whole host of Christian workers who had devoted themselves independently to witnessing among their own people without any affiliations, financial support, or training. My path crossed more and more with these people who weren't directly a part of India Gospel League but who were looking for help at various levels. I would do my best to encourage them, pray with them, and support them. I began to challenge them to concentrate on villages that were unreached. They were coming to me one-by-one, and I started spending more time with these individuals.

Gideon was one of these. His conversion occurred when he was seriously ill and had little hope of survival. A nearby pastor received a prompting from God to go to room 108 at the local hospital. When he did, the pastor found Gideon on his deathbed. Gideon said, "If I am healed, I will commit my life to Christ and give my full time to share Him with others." The pastor began praying, and at that moment, Gideon was miraculously healed.

From that day forward, Gideon was full of zeal. He started preaching and teaching, and soon he had a group of believers around him. That is when I first came into contact with him. Encouraging, assisting and helping Gideon was a rewarding experience for me.

I was able to find partners for him who helped fund a Life Center (church building) in his village. This particular church was located on a garbage dump, so India Gospel League leadership referred to it as "the church on the dump." Believe it or not, from that "dump" a whole host of outreaches have grown up, including seventy-five new church planters sent out to other villages. In the years following, Gideon became a regional coordinator. Gideon's two sons have become pastors themselves and oversee two additional regions of church planting effort in India. Just from what I know, I would say at least two hundred churches have sprung up from the work God did in Gideon's life in just twenty years.

By 1990, there were probably about one hundred such people (like Gideon) that I was regularly praying and working with, and these new relationships were increasingly capturing my focus. In November of that year, India Gospel League hosted its first pastors' conference in an effort to bring these faithful believers together. Around a hundred and fifty attended. While many were pastors, others were itinerant workers for the gospel.

This conference, developed with the help of an American pastor I had met on a trip to the U.S., Pastor Claude from Ohio, had the following goals in mind: to provide the attendees with encouragement, inspiration, motivation, theological training, practical ministry tools, and of course, great fellowship with each other. We also aimed to give them great food, as these pastors were used to living on the bare minimums of life. We thought it would be a blessing if, for this single week, they could eat the best meals they'd had all year!

Pastor Claude's specialty was in master planning, goal setting, and the training that accompanies such things in a church context. He came to India accepting my invitation to help our pastors learn how to set clear goals for their ministries, develop objectives, and really see the churches of India grow, all by the Holy Spirit's power. The approach of strategic planning and goal setting was novel to them, as these concepts (particularly in ministry work) had not yet become common.

Many of these men would share the gospel faithfully, but they typically wouldn't plan ahead for much. The mentality was more to plant seeds and then leave the results to the Spirit, without any clear objectives or outcome goals. In that first conference, we discussed the fact that there is nothing wrong with praying intentionally and specifically for plans and progress. That discussion proved to be transformative.

In a practical sense, it meant that instead of simply voicing broad hopes ("I plan to share the gospel in this village."), we encouraged more actionable specifics ("I plan to train two people for evangelism, and then take them out to a village to speak with every resident on Fridays."). The more we challenged pastors to get intentional about their planning, the more results we started to see. They would start with the vision God had put on their hearts (such as discipleship training, caring for lepers, or reaching out to children), and then they would be encouraged to plan back through all the necessary steps that would lead to their vision coming to pass.

A GOAL TOGETHER

The next year, I felt the Lord calling this new group of loosely affiliated ministers to a unified goal—a cohesive Great Commission plan that would touch the least reached areas of India. Still, even near my home village where India Gospel League had been born more than forty years prior, there were areas that had no church and, consequently, no ongoing Christian witness.

In 1992, at the third pastors' conference, I laid out a plan God had laid on my heart—a joint goal of planting one thousand churches by the year 2000. We determined that a church would be defined as at least twenty baptized adults meeting weekly for worship. Combining our effort, and yet with each church planter maintaining his own autonomy, could we attempt such a goal? We knew the ramifications for the kingdom of God would be immeasurable. We named our plan "Vision 2000" (a term still in wide use today to describe the church planting movement in India). For a pastor to join Vision 2000, he would commit to start a new work in an unreached village – *every year.*

What we didn't know is that this vision would light a fire that would change *far more* than a thousand villages!

God was doing something extraordinary in the hearts of these independent church planters. My presupposition had always been that the "normal" way of growing new leaders would be for India Gospel League to select them, train them theologically, and then send them out to the field. But without any external organization at all, God was raising illiterate, impoverished, newly-converted people without formal training to start churches in areas where no churches had been started before. There were far more people like Pastor Gideon than I would have ever imagined. It was as if we were back in New Testament times, with Jesus calling His very unqualified group of disciples together and sending them out with nothing but His power and His Word!

I immediately changed my focus from growing the

organization to equipping these people. We closed down our Bible school so that instead of bringing these church plant-ers to an institution for training, we could concentrate on getting training opportunities out to them, in the villages, in their own context.

Within a year, Vision 2000 had grown beyond our own cul-tural group. We had to have translators at the annual pastors' conferences that followed (India is a land with fourteen major language groups and more than 1,600 local dialects). Our small ministry in Tamil Nadu blossomed quickly and unexpectedly into a movement of the Holy Spirit throughout South India.

For me this movement became a journey that reflected Dr. Henry Blackaby's maxim from the *Experiencing God* Bible study: "Find out were God is working, and join Him in that work!" And God was working indeed—not through the institutions and structures I would have expected, but in the remote villages, in the hearts of average people called to be fishers of men, just like Peter and John two millennia ago.

I recall one illiterate woman, completely uneducated and quite elderly. When I was introduced to her, I learned that she had established sixteen groups that were in the process of becoming churches in sixteen different villages! I asked her how this was possible, how she was winning so many people to Christ. She replied: "When I see people I feel I should witness to, I open my Bible, put my finger on a verse, and ask *them* to read it! As they read the verse aloud, I pray for God's wisdom to expound on it, and how I can use that passage to tell them about Jesus."

Another man named Stephen had essentially planted a church and didn't realize it. He came to me looking for some support to provide Bibles for new believers, and that's how we connected. I visited his fledgling congregation, helped him with the needed Bibles, and connected him to India Gospel League's network. From there, we provided a bicycle to increase the range of his ministry and some musical instruments to begin developing church worship. Two years later, we also helped him build a Life Center. After recognizing that he was, in fact, a "church planter," Stephen went on to help coordinate additional church planting efforts in surrounding areas. Since that time, he has been instrumental in developing fifty other church planters to send to nearby regions.

AND GOD WAS WORKING INDEED— NOT THROUGH THE INSTITUTIONS I WOULD HAVE EXPECTED, BUT IN THE REMOTE VILLAGES.

I remember one village where a church of two hundred people began based on the testimony of three individuals: an alcoholic man who was vomiting blood, suddenly healed; an elderly woman who had broken her hip, suddenly healed; and a young boy, eleven years old, who was given a gift of passionate prayer for people. That boy had Down syndrome, but when he prayed, people would get well! I recall so vividly that when this boy heard I was in his village, he wanted to pray for me. I knelt down so that he could put his hands on my head. He prayed one of the most beautiful prayers I've ever heard!

I came away from the village that day thinking about how God uses unlikely vessels to do his work: this preteen boy, a man given to alcohol, and an elderly woman being used to start a church in an unreached village! It proved to me there is certainly a place for everyone to be used in God's kingdom.

GROWING RANKS

The numbers of people affiliating themselves with the movement grew rapidly, and the number of churches being planted as a result of this new approach quickly surpassed the one thousand we had originally set out to establish. As a group, we decided to revise our goal upwards, believing that we should work toward the establishment of five thousand churches in India. Then in 1996, we started moving forward in Sri Lanka, the island nation off the southern coast of India, with the same overall strategy. Our plan was to bring together the independent church planters God had already raised up on the island, help them set goals, and provide them with as much training and as many resources as we could. Many of these brave Christian workers committed to reach out to at least one additional village every year, in concert with the Vision 2000 movement in India.

By the year 2000, we celebrated not one thousand, not five thousand, but more than *twenty thousand* new churches planted (in some of the most needy areas imaginable). A movement had begun, not from our own strategy, not from our own organization, not from our own plans. It was a *kairos* moment. India Gospel League simply had joined a great movement that the Holy Spirit had already initiated.

Today many of those early church planters have trained scores more under them, and the list of church plants springing out from India Gospel League has grown well beyond 85,000. Many young congregations meet in villages that have never before had a gospel witness in their midst!

I could have missed all of this. I could have missed the divine opportunity to partner with faithful laborers like these.

It would have been easy for me to focus in on India Gospel League as it once was, to work hard to grow the Bible school or other ministry outreaches in the state of Tamil Nadu, and to completely miss the great harvest God was about to bring in. It would have been easy for us to stick with our traditions, with what had worked in the past, to go the "safer route."

Thankfully, God had other plans.

———————————

HOW MANY?

There is no biblical minimum for what constitutes a church, but as we count churches in India, we are looking specifically for groups of twenty or more baptized adult believers. Groups less than this number are considered to be discipleship groups.

FOR FURTHER DISCUSSION

1. Why do you think Christians, even those with faith in God, are so tempted to "play it safe" in decisions? Have you ever taken a risk in following God's path? What was the result?

2. If your church needed a paradigm shift, how do you think it would come about? How would you personally respond to it?

3. Do you think you have ever missed a "*kairos* moment" opportunity? If so, why?

CHAPTER 3

HOW DO YOU KNOW?

The fastest way to kill a sweeping movement is to try to control it. That's one reason India Gospel League doesn't have administrative control over our church planters, and we don't want to. They aren't "ours" to begin with! If we were to begin calling the shots, paying the salaries, and installing the leaders, I believe we would take this *kairos* moment opportunity and box it into human parameters.

Now, of course I'm not against organization. As you get to know India Gospel League, you'll see aspects of our ministry (medical outreach, children's sponsorships, training programs, economic development initiatives, etc.) that are highly organized. And most certainly our attempts at serving and equipping local leaders are well organized. But when it comes to the church planting itself—the gospel movement now transforming villages across South Asia—we don't want to get in the way of what God is doing. We want to join Him in *His* work!

This approach leads to an important question then, which is constantly on my heart and in my prayers. *How do you or I know when God is doing something new?*

How do we sense additional *kairos* moments and not get stuck in traditions of our own? How do we know when we've entered the "Samaritan village" ready for spiritual transformation, or when we've entered the kind wherein Jesus instructed the disciples to "shake the dust off" of their feet as they leave?

I don't have a full answer to that question because in every case I think some wrestling in prayer is necessary, and seeking wisdom and counsel is critical as well. But I would start by asking God to *develop in our hearts a kingdom mentality*. Once we are thinking in terms of advancing His kingdom instead of our own ideas, God can open our eyes to things we had not previously seen. That's when our horizons expand.

We can begin by asking these questions:

- How, today, is the kingdom of God growing?
- How is it being established in new places?
- How was it established in my area and in my life?

Perhaps by contrasting the present and the past, we can begin to see how God is working now and how His purposes are being fulfilled around us. This contrast may lead us to some very different conclusions about methodology or practice than would our traditions or personal biases.

Here is an illustration from India. I report with some sorrow in my heart that there are still large Christian organizations working in the mission field that do not recognize the efforts of independent church planters. Some groups are still operating under structures and assumptions that were established more than a century ago. They fail to see they could join God in His work through a means different than what they expect or are willing to offer. The result is that a tremendous amount of money and missionary effort is either wasted or far less effective than it could be.

The Pharisees made a similar error with Christ. Jesus was nothing like the Messiah they expected, so most of them rejected His claims out of hand, even when confronted with His most powerful miracles and His most profound teachings. Their experience, and that of modern Christian organizations that continue to operate with an old paradigm, demonstrates how easy it is for any of us to box ourselves in, to only accept that which we have anticipated, and to miss the powerful presence of God!

In humility perhaps we should begin by praying, *"Lord, show us how You are working today. Help us discern those things we should hold on to, and those things You intend to change. And, help us surrender our preconceived notions so we can fully respond to your Holy Spirit's leading!"*

KAIROS MOMENTS TO COME

I don't want to repeat devastating mistakes that others have made or cling to my own newfound "traditions" or expectations. I also don't want to begin looking at how God was moving in India in the 1990s and the 2000s as a blueprint for how He will always work in India. Things *will* change. New *kairos* moments *will* be ahead, new opportunities for the kingdom that no one yet foresees.

As a leader I must ask myself, "How can I stay on top of what's coming next? How can I remain sensitive to the Holy Spirit when He redirects us again?" As I ask myself these questions, I have to suspect that pastors across the the world face the same struggle.

One obvious way to meet this challenge is to stay rooted in God's Word by reading and rereading the New Testament, particularly the book of Acts. I do everything I can to encourage pastors and church planters to stay open to what the Holy Spirit is saying and doing and never to rest on human strategies or ideals. You and I must never suspect that our own ingenuity or giftedness has brought us to where we are in ministry. Instead we must acknowledge that we are completely beholden to the Lord for His gracious work among us and through us. If we deviate from the path He opens before us, we will almost certainly forfeit our involvement in whatever *kairos* moments lie ahead.

Another way I am addressing this challenge is to spend more and more of my time investing in the future leaders of Indian and Sri Lankan churches, helping them discern God's purposes for their communities and helping them see and understand *kairos* moments. More than anything else I am involved in today, I see this as the most strategic in helping the kingdom of God advance for many years to come, long after my own personal mission is complete.

Rather than a few large organizations and high-profile leaders attempting to discern God's will for a nation, imagine hundreds or even thousands of local Christian leaders, all listening to the Holy Spirit, seeking divine opportunities, and being sensitive to His ultimate leadership. This vision means trusting in God to lead rather than men. This approach requires faith and a humble attitude, like John the Baptist, who said, "He (Jesus) must become greater, I must become less" (John 3:30).

Are we willing to trust the Holy Spirit's leadership of a *new* Christian movement? Or somewhere in our hearts is there a strong, unspoken desire to step in and show Him how to do it? To keep things the way we like them, the way they've always been?

FROM TWENTY TO SIX THOUSAND

In 1988 my "right hand man"—Pastor Benny—joined our team. He came to lead our Bible school programs and started faithfully conducting this part of our ministry. He had worked previously with Operation Mobilization and had graduated from seminary. He seemed to be an obvious choice for our ministry. But when we recognized the *kairos* moment and decided to shut down the Bible school, where did that leave Pastor Benny?

At first he focused on how to take Bible school training and make it available to pastors in the villages—men like Stephen and Gideon, who though full of zeal, needed to grow in biblical knowledge. It didn't make sense to pull them out of the field, out of their villages, so they could receive training. So

Pastor Benny and a team started taking the training out to them in the form of regional conferences, modular study courses, and local accountability groups.

> ONCE WE ARE THINKING IN TERMS OF ADVANCING HIS KINGDOM INSTEAD OF OUR OWN IDEAS, GOD CAN OPEN OUR EYES TO THINGS WE HAD NOT PREVIOUSLY SEEN.

Soon Pastor Benny was no longer training twenty young people at a time (as he did when we had the Bible school open). Instead he was investing in hundreds of men who were already active in ministry and aggressively planting additional churches. After seeing the success of this approach, we then initiated local lay leader training programs for youth, women, and men to deepen the spiritual life of the blossoming Indian church.

Pastor Benny is now developing a network for advanced theological training. He is intent on seeing five hundred "trainers" raised up—fifty in ten different language groups—so these trainers can offer biblical education to thousands of future pastors. The impact? Almost incalculable!

Currently more than two hundred training meetings are occurring across South Asia each month. That's 2,400 per year! And, at this point in time, more than 6,000 pastors look to Pastor Benny as their teacher and mentor while tens of thousands of lay people are participating in our local leadership and discipleship programs.

I don't report all these numbers to brag on Pastor Benny. Rather I offer his story as an example of how critical it is for all of us to be willing to respond to *kairos* moments. What if we hadn't changed? What if we had played it safe and kept our Bible school open? The "good" we were doing would have prevented us from the "great" that God had in mind.

I'm sure Pastor Benny would have remained faithful to his work in either case. But God wanted to multiply the kingdom in ways we had never anticipated and would not have "strategized." This story is just one example of why seeing and interpreting the *kairos* moment for our time is so important.

MISSING POTENTIAL

It is not only in the realm of mission strategy or pastoral leadership that *kairos* moments may be missed. Sometimes, our cultural assumptions, prejudices, or societal norms cause us to overlook how the Holy Spirit is moving, or *through whom* He is moving.

Here's a heartbreaking illustration of what I mean: some time ago the *New York Times* ran an article entitled: "100 Million Are Missing." Demographic scientists can usually predict how many males and females will be born, and this article pointed out that as many as 100 million little girls are missing from today's generation worldwide. While some of this disparity can be accounted for by medical factors, the reality still very obvious - many families have purposely killed their daughters.

India and China are responsible for many millions of these missing girls. Sons are more desirable and wanted for a host of cultural and financial reasons. When an ultrasound shows a child is a female, mothers often, sadly, elect for abortion. Thousands of other girl babies, though carried to full-term, are left neglected and exposed to the elements, to die a secret death.

I contend that women's ministry is another opportunity in God's kingdom work that the church has been slow to embrace (at least, in my culture this has been the case). History shows that women have always played a key role in the growth of God's kingdom, when God began great works of His Spirit. A study of historic spiritual awakenings shows that women, in the early stages, were often just as active as men in sharing the gospel, praying fervently, and meeting the needs of their communities. Sadly, as the excitement of revival cooled and the activity turned from "movement" into "structure," women were often left out.

The Moravian revival of the eighteenth century is a classic example. It was through this move of God at the first Protestant missionaries moved out to reach the entire world. The whole movement was undergirded by a twenty-four-hour prayer vigil for the unreached that is said to have lasted *over a hundred years*. Among the great pioneers of the Moravian Missionary Movement, many were women–making great personal sacrifices, pushing forward the front lines of the gospel's advance.

Another example comes from John and Charles Wesley, who were leaders in the spiritual awakening that transformed England and America during the late 1700s and early 1800s. The key to the great commitment of the Wesley brothers, it is said, was their godly mother Susanna. She spent extended time each day in earnest prayer. Along with that, she also found time to teach and nurture each of her nine children!

Mrs. Wesley taught more than two hundred people every week in prayer meetings, which she led in her husband's parish. John Wesley recruited women leaders for the small groups that he called "classes." When asked about this, Wesley would say, "Since God uses women in the conversion of sinners, who am I that I should withstand God?"

> **YOU AND I MUST NEVER SUSPECT THAT OUR OWN INGENUITY OR GIFTEDNESS HAS BROUGHT US TO WHERE WE ARE IN MINISTRY.**

A recent law against conversion that is promulgated in South India metes out greater punishment to those converting women. Why? Because it has been recognized that wherever women have come to the Lord in substantial numbers, entire communities have experienced significant transformation in every dimension of life.

Several Indian women have led the fray against the darkness of ignorance, superstition and dark practices bringing about deliverance and change. Pandit Ramabai, one of the great female social reformers in Indian history, serves as a classic example of the contribution women can make to the growth of churches and the improvement of society. Countless women in like manner are playing a key part in local community transformations today, sharing the gospel, creating educational opportunities, and taking bold steps forward to a brighter future. They continue to pay a high price on account of their faith in Christ.

I am excited to report that the South Asian church is experiencing a great surge among and through women. Their unique giftedness in developing and sustaining relationships with other women has built bridges that God is using to reach communities. (Needless to say, women seem to possess the innate ability to build deeper and more meaningful relationships than men – I think this may be true in any culture!) Empowered women have been observed to play a major role in development programs of the churches, particularly because they excel in compassion and love.

India Gospel League has been pioneering women-focused missions for more than five decades. Since it is estimated that more than two-thirds of all Bible-believing Christians are women, we believe it is critical to see women trained, engaged and empowered! Excluding them from evangelistic work results in indescribable loss of church potential, in any part of the world.

Women touched and changed by the gospel have the power to transform a community (think of the Samaritan woman in John 4, or Mary Magdalene, or so many others mentioned in Scripture). In the past few years, thousands of South Asian women have responded to God's love and the claims of Christ in their lives. They have been released from the torments of centuries-old cultural prejudices. They have been liberated from their low self-image and crippling fears, freeing them to share the gospel with others.

I wholeheartedly believe that God is using them as agents of healing in our society, helping those who have been neglected, oppressed, and forgotten. They are catalysts bringing about seismic change and remarkable transformation. (Unfortunately, in much of the traditional church structure, this move of God is not recognized yet, and thus, few provisions for women's ministry are made.)

Sensing that God was doing something new in and among the women of our culture, we began to ask how we could adequately train, empower, and equip them as ambassadors for Christ.

In 1998, God prompted us to begin "Women With a Mission" to accomplish precisely that. India Gospel League initiated plans to mobilize 10,000 women – equipping them for evangelism, leadership and discipleship.

Before the end of 1999, close to 3,000 women were identified and recruited for ongoing training. Since then, this group of leaders has grown to more than 5,300 (as of 2016). These are women who take a lead role in both the practical and spiritual growth of others, who lead small groups of women in their communities to make an impact. They study God's Word, determine what compassionate care or assistance they could offer their village, make plans to extend the gospel into new areas, tackle needed economic development initiatives, provide encouragement to one another and, through the local church, serve in many ministry roles.

For some cultures, and even for some denominations, an emphasis on women's ministry leadership is uncomfortable, and pushes up against their assumptions and preferences. Certainly in South Asia it is out-of-the-ordinary to see village women taking leadership responsibility for the good of their communities, forming prayer groups, initiating social change, and sharing the gospel. And yet we see the same pattern playing out here as has been clearly seen throughout Scripture and church history: God works through unlikely people, in unexpected ways.

He surprises us with *kairos* moments that we would never have seen coming, opportunities that no strategic planner would have anticipated.

Of course, these matters deserve humble prayer. But they also require prompt obedience. We wouldn't want to miss a window that God opens just because we are so used to doing things a certain way.

———————————

HOW MANY?

We estimate that to finish the job of reaching every region of India with the gospel, church planting movements need to be initiated in about 200 additional regions. Each region includes several thousand villages, and among them millions of people!

FOR FURTHER DISCUSSION

1. How are you seeking God for wisdom regarding the opportunities around you? How are you listening?

2. Participating in *kairos* moments requires humble honesty, particularly if we discover that God is moving through methods or styles different from our own. How would you react if you realized that your organization, church style, or approach to life was a hindrance to participating in a divine moment?

3. What would it mean for you to trust the Holy Spirit's leadership?

CHAPTER 4

NORTH AND BEYOND

More than two thousand "people groups" in India still need a living church.

To say it differently, more than two thousand different groups of people are what mission agencies call "unreached." (People groups are different than geographic regions. In some regions, a people group may have access to the gospel, but their neighbors of a different ethnicity in the same location do not.)

Shockingly, this statistic means that despite the dramatic advance of the Christian church in South Asia over the past few decades, nearly one billion people in India still qualify as being unreached with the gospel.

One billion people who need "living water" from the Savior.

This statistic is changing today for the better as hundreds of new congregations are being planted every month. Hundreds of thousands of children too are now able to attend gospel clubs that provide them with the joy of knowing Jesus and hope for their future. And tens of thousands of young people are answering the call to vocational ministry, many to go to the unreached. Yet compared to the sheer numeric need, these advances represent only a healthy start to sharing the Good News with South Asia. The lion's share of the work remains to be done.

WHAT IF YOUR NATION OR YOUR CITY IS ABOUT TO EXPERIENCE A KAIROS MOMENT? ARE YOU READY?

I pray that I will live to see the day when every one of India's 650,000+ rural communities has its own Bible-believing congregation. I pray that one day soon every man, woman, and child in South Asia will have the opportunity to respond to the gospel and have freedom and access to join a local church family.

To see this desire come to pass, however, we need much more than human effort and much more than a few additional offerings donated to global missions. We need the presence and power of God at work through a *kairos* moment, and that is precisely what God has sent to us in recent years. Extraordinary opportunities, open hearts, willing hearers, new laborers for the harvest fields, and clear direction from the Holy Spirit are all in play, today, across the region. God is answering the prayers of His people, bringing light and openness to places where darkness has reigned for generations.

In the early days of India Gospel League, most of the activity we saw happening was in the south and central regions of India. In the northern and eastern regions, there was less of a foundation for church multiplication. But then we began to see God raising up independent church planters in these locations as well, many of whom didn't realize an outsider might call them a "church planter" (they were just following the New Testament!). And just as we experienced in the south and central regions of India, these individuals began crossing our path and coming to us for assistance.

KINGDOM CONNECTIONS

In the early 2000s, India Gospel League began receiving help requests from Bihar, a state in northeast India that once was dubbed the "graveyard of missions." (In 2001, the census reported far less than one percent of the population there claimed any form of Christianity.) We wanted to encourage church planting in this area, and we had been praying about it.

While I was traveling to Bihar to meet with a few pastors beginning ministry work there, I received a call out of the blue from a pastor named "Loyall" in Texas. As a result of some mission classes his church had hosted, his mission team selected Bihar as a new area to focus some of their prayer and giving. Pastor Loyall was calling me to see if India Gospel League had any interest in the region or any connections there. He was very specific: *"We want to get involved in church planting in Bihar!"* Soon thereafter, I invited Pastor Loyall and the lead pastor of the church, Pastor Joe, to come to India to see the context of the work we were about to engage in.

In India, I told Joe, "I want to give you a proposal to reach Bihar.

It's a big one, probably bigger than what one church could do." The next day he reported that he didn't sleep a wink that night and by morning was ready to make a commitment to go for it. His church had a relatively small congregation, but they went ahead and took on a multi-hundred-thousand-dollar challenge to fund the strategic mission advance I'd proposed. It was unlike any step of faith this church had taken before!

The results?

In just four years, more than three hundred new churches were started in Bihar. This outcome was a result of the responsive generosity of this pastor and his congregation linked together with the sacrificial commitment of hundreds of church plant-ers boldly stepping into new and difficult territory. And God gets the glory!

Many other churches have partnered with us (both prior to and following the experience noted above) - adopting entire regions and helping us plant thousands of churches in a similar way.

Stories like this one are repeating all across South Asia and all across the world. The fields are "ripe for harvest" (John 4:35) for those who are paying attention, who are engaging directly in the work of the Great Commission.

Since that time, in Bihar, Jharkhand, and other regions across North and Central India, God has allowed us to minister encouragement and provide training for hundreds of young leaders in the most remote, tribal, and even hostile (to the gospel) areas. In fact, after a recent earthquake, some of our leaders ended up serving the pastors of Nepal (along the northern border of India), which has led to a new regional partnership to train pastors and spread the church planting movement into that nation. Once again, a *kairos* moment was upon us, and our team had to act deliberately to change our way of thinking, to enlarge our expectations, and to begin serving these brothers and sisters in what we would call "remote regions."

Are there additional risks? Yes!

Are these people in different language groups? Yes!

Is there opposition from radicals? Yes!

Is there a lack of resources? Yes!

Is there a great need for theological training in young churches? Yes!

Is the church growing? Exponentially!

Kairos moments like this one feel like a page in the book of Acts, as if we are traveling right alongside Paul, Barnabas, Peter, or Timothy. Do you remember Peter's vision on the rooftop, when God told him to begin ministry to the Gentiles? Or when Philip miraculously met the Ethiopian just as he was reading a prophecy about Jesus? It seemed in that day and age that God was at work all over the place, connecting His people to gospel opportunities they would never have imagined possible.

We can get so used to the way things are that we lose vision for the way things ought to be. You may live half-a-world away from Indian village churches, but is God any less interested in your city hearing the gospel? Or about His power being displayed through your local church? Are there still people around you who have never heard about Jesus or who have never come face-to-face with Christian compassion?

God obviously does move at certain times and in certain places and in special ways. But what if He really desires to move in your community, with the same power that He is using to transform lives in India? Or with the same intensity as was seen during the Great Awakenings in American history? Or with the same Spirit-leadership that was demonstrated among the first-century church in Jerusalem? What if your nation or your city is about to experience a *kairos* moment? Are you ready?

Many of my international friends who visit India note that it feels a bit like stepping into the book of Acts. I appreciate what they are saying, and I agree. I welcome you to come and see for yourself (note Appendix A).

But my challenge here goes deeper than that. Yes, God is doing amazing things here. But what if you didn't need to travel away from home to experience a *kairos* moment? What if God was working dramatically and obviously in *your* context, in your church? What if people who visited your community left saying things like, "This feels like the book of Acts?"

THE THIRD WAVE

One way I like to explain God's amazing work in India today is by calling it the "third wave" of mission activity in this culture (a similar wave pattern can be seen in other cultures as well, throughout history). One of the primary reasons India Gospel League has had such wide-ranging impact is not because of our own power or brilliance or money. Instead it's because we have ridden the third wave and continue to do so!

Here is what I mean when discussing "waves" of mission activity:

- **Wave 1:** Cross-cultural or foreign mission efforts introduce people to the gospel. They respond in faith, and the seeds of a Christian movement are planted. At this stage, local churches are led by outsiders. This approach represents the framework of "traditional missions" in the West for the past two hundred years, with large missionary sending agencies that transplant missionary families from one culture to another in order to plant churches or conduct direct ministry to the population.

- **Wave 2:** The foreign mission workers begin training local leaders for the churches so the leadership of the church becomes indigenous. The workers from the first wave continue their presence and involvement and sometimes continue to provide leadership, strategy, and resources. However, the strategy begins to shift away from transplanting more missionaries cross-culturally and toward empowering and equipping local leaders.

- **Wave 3:** The indigenous pastors set forth their own

strategy, provide their own leadership, and operate based on their own resources. Wave 3 church planting is entirely indigenous, taking on the character and style of the local culture into which it was born. Existing cross-cultural mission groups may be looked at as peer-level partners in getting various projects done, but all of the leadership is provided in-country and in-culture.

To me it is very obvious that India (and other nations in South Asia) entered the third wave a few decades ago, and that agencies or churches still focused on the first two waves are becoming less effective on the ground. This news may be uncomfortable for some, particularly if they still have large systems built to sustain wave one or wave two activities, and strong relationships with people still engaged in that type of work. But to them I say as Jesus said, "Lift up your eyes" (John 4:35) and see what God is doing. The fact that much of the world is experiencing the third wave is wonderful news. The seeds planted in previous generations are now bearing fruit, and millions are hearing the gospel as a result.

HOPE IN THE DARK TIMES

Years ago many thought that nothing was happening with Christianity in China because the communists had thrown out all of the missionaries. Later it was discovered that a vast network of underground churches was growing exponentially during that time and millions had come to know Jesus personally. God was at still at work, the gospel was still spreading, and the Holy Spirit was still moving in those dark times!

Today we are hearing stories of how God is moving powerfully in the Muslim world, where the doors to Christian activity have been slammed shut and where even discussing the New Testament could land a person in prison or worse. Even in the midst of war, terrorism, and persecution, the work of the Holy Spirit continues there as well.

In reflecting over the past few decades on how God has been at work, I've come to believe that it is up to the church to recognize where God is moving and to boldly obey what the Scripture says to do in response. Is God moving in the USA? Yes! Russia? Yes! Australia? Yes! Europe? Yes!

God is able to work *through you* in your region. Will you take His call seriously? Will you step forward as a Great Commission visionary, even in the midst of deep darkness?

Revelation 22:17 is a clear example of how the Spirit works in partnership with the church to share the gospel invitation with the world. "The Spirit and the Bride say, 'Come.' And let the one who hears say, 'Come.' And let the one who is thirsty come; let the one who desires take the water of life without price."

That invitation knows no national borders. It isn't limited to any geography or culture. The Holy Spirit is doing His work. But I wonder, are we doing ours?

HOW MANY?

India is about one third the geographic size of the United States, but it is home to four times the number of people! There are more than 1.3 billion Indians alive today, and the nation is on track to surpass China as the most populous on earth within a few years.

FOR FURTHER DISCUSSION

1. Has there ever been an obvious and widespread *kairos* moment in your culture? Have you ever studied the history of the Christian movement among your people group?

2. If you were a church leader in India today, what might concern you about the rapid growth of the church in the region? What problems might surface that would need attention and prayer?

3. Think of the various mission activities you have been a part of over the years. Which "wave" were those connected with?

CHAPTER 5

OF THE SOIL

W e often invite pastors from other nations to share in some of our training conferences, particularly those who are willing to teach theological or leadership development material to rural pastors. We see this as a great way to expose Indian pastors to the larger framework of how God is working worldwide. It also is a way to help pastors (like Loyall and Joe from Texas) catch the vision of what their partnership with indigenous Indian pastors could look like.

This cross-cultural ministry isn't without its mishaps and humor, however. One American pastor visited with us and was planning to share some church growth principles with our village pastors. After he arrived he realized he needed to change his notes because they included a section on detailing the right amount of parking space needed for new church buildings! Growing a church in suburban America is quite a bit different than doing so in rural Maharashtra! We joked with him about a culturally equivalent need, that churches in India would build extra space to handle all the footwear of the worshipers (because it is customary in India to remove one's shoes before entering church).

This story illustrates an important reality about mission work. No matter how intriguing or convincing a foreigners may be, they face a significant limitation. They are not "indigenous" to the local culture, the land, or the language. By definition, they are different. Their worldview, assumptions, and approach differ greatly from those of the local believers.

Some of you were raised in a context where "foreign missions" involved gospel sharing efforts in countries other than yours. The term implied you would step out of your own culture and into someone else's, hoping to share the Good News and Christian compassion with those who were uninformed of the gospel. Then, upon the completion of your experience, you would step back into your home culture and share about all that you learned.

Some faithful servants of Christ took foreign missions a step further, committing themselves to leave the comforts of home on a semi-permanent basis to set up mission stations in other countries from which to minister to the least reached. This commitment has been an important part of the gospel's advance into many cultures around the world, and it began with the Lord himself, who stepped down from His heavenly throne and entered into human culture.

INDIGENOUS LEADERSHIP AND VISION TO ASSIST

In spite of the gains of these foreign mission efforts, there exists a challenge today that many denominations and agencies have been slow in addressing. It is, in short, the need for *indigenous leadership* of local churches.

The second part of the challenge is to have an *intentional vision to assist* (rather than direct) these leaders. Why? Unless a local community itself "owns" a given mission, it will not grow to maturity. The ways to assist and partner are many, but the aim of this assistance must be to serve the local pastor's vision for reaching his community.

Without indigenous leadership in the driver's seat, church plants made by individuals and agencies on the outside of the local culture continue to exist on some form of foreign life support—with foreign boards, denominations, or missionaries leading the strategy. In my experience, this approach to spreading the gospel becomes extremely unhealthy over time and often detrimental to the work of the Holy Spirit.

This is one area where sensitivity to *kairos* moments may lead us away from traditional ways of thinking. For example, if you evaluate the average mission program in the West, it is usually discussed in terms of leading and administrating, which includes funding trained (usually foreign) workers to travel and work in a new culture where they learn the language, share the gospel in the way they believe is right, and begin training local leaders. A few places in the world need this approach, but it is slow and costly. This is an old paradigm that needs significant revision for the 21st century!

To reach the world in this generation, I believe we must think in new terms. What if the lesson India Gospel League learned in 1992—that God is raising up laborers for His harvest field in ways we never expected—is actually a trend happening across the world?

I like to call what we're involved in *parakletic* mission, which means "coming alongside" the native believers, finding out what God is doing through them, and then running along with them to serve and share. Embracing a *parakletic* approach to mission means taking leadership books and church growth methodologies with a grain of salt and trusting the Holy Spirit to take the lead in ways we can't foresee. It means caring far less about church worship style, evangelistic methods, and "brand name," and far more about the advancement of God's kingdom.

I suppose my thoughts here could sound a bit too absolute. My intention is not to minimize the work of the many devoted gospel laborers across the world still engaged in the traditional approach. There is still a place for these cross-cultural missions, of course. But if you could see what I see, I think you would agree with me: the global church is missing some amazing *kairos* moment opportunities right now. Our resources are not being allocated where they can make the greatest impact, and we are operating with a host of human strategies (sometimes in competition with each other) rather than really seeking God for His way of reaching the world right now. Missionary traditions and funding models have become so entrenched in both overseas mission-sending agencies and local church mission committees that needed changes have been painfully slow in coming.

As an example, I recently heard a statistic from the Issachar

Initiative, a group interested in completing the Great Commission task, regarding the amount of church resources combined that are invested in reaching the least-reached areas on earth. The amount? *Less than one percent* is being allocated to reach more than two billion souls in desperately impoverished and difficult fields. (Source: issacharinitiative.org)

NEW QUESTIONS

Would it be dangerous to ask, "Lord, what are You doing today, and how can we join You?"

What if that question leads us away from business as usual? What if it means we have less say on how the work of God is administrated? Or how much credit is given to our denomination or ministry organization? What if it means that our paradigm shifts somehow, away from established norms?

Try the following as a thought experiment.

Imagine that you sense God's call to reach out to a certain people group in another nation. Here are some of the questions people are accustomed to asking:

• How hard would it be for me to learn the language?

• Do I need to attend seminary before I can go?

• Does the location have familiar stores, restaurants, and health care options?

- What immunizations will I need?

- Could I go on a short-term trip to see the lay of the land first?

- How could I start a church in that culture?

Now imagine the same calling from the Holy Spirit but a different set of questions:

- Are there local churches already inside or nearby this culture?

- How could I get to know the local pastors and find ways to serve them?

- What needs do the local pastors identify that God might allow me to meet?

- Is it helpful for me to visit or live there, or should I partner with them in another way?

- What unique work is God doing there, and how can I pray for and support it?

AN EXAMPLE FROM SRI LANKA

The church planting movement that began in India in 1992, which we refer to as "Vision 2000" on the field, was simply our recognition of what the Holy Spirit was already doing in India. God led us not to direct the movement's pastors but instead to serve them and to look for ways to help them establish their own ministries with strong theology, solid planning, and a fellowship of like-hearted Christian leaders. We weren't conducting the movement's frontline evangelism—the churches being planted were (and still are). Our role was to equip and enable what their leadership determined to do.

In the late 1990s, when India Gospel League began assisting the local Sri Lankan churches, we crossed our first national boundary as an organization. We did not send Indians over the Gulf of Mannar to begin evangelizing or planting churches. Instead, we recognized who the indigenous church leaders were and began training and resourcing them to the best of our ability.

We continue to conduct some cross-cultural leadership training, but not direct ministry work. The churches being planted on Sri Lanka today aren't "ours," and we aren't administrating them from some foreign office in India. The leadership of the Sri Lankan churches comes from the Sri Lankan churches!

INDIGENEITY

We are doing our best to "practice what we preach" on indigenous leadership. If you are familiar at all with the history of India, you know we are really a nation compromised of many people groups and tribes. There are fourteen major languages spoken (Hindi, Marathi, Tamil, and English are a few of them) and hundreds of local dialects. The culture of North India is very different from that in South India, and significant cultural differences exist even state-to-state and region-to-region.

Because of our nation's diverse language and culture, we practice the principle of indigeneity as much as possible. We don't want to transplant leaders from their culture and people group to go and lead among others. Instead, our vision is for every people group to have its own homegrown leadership team to share the gospel, serve the needy, and advance the kingdom of Jesus.

A recent example of this dynamic was brought to my attention during the translation of our children's materials, which we offer to churches throughout India to use in evangelism and discipleship efforts. As we translate, we have to do adaptive translation to the local contexts or, even better, find authors from those cultures to originate content. Some local leaders in North India remarked to us in previous years that the artistic images and music we sent along with the curriculum looked and sounded "South Indian" stylistically. Reworking every aspect of the materials to better fit their context was an expensive and complex proposition, but we are doing our best to adapt to it. If we want our material to genuinely serve the churches in that region, we have to adapt.

AUTOCHTHONOUS

My friends often tease me for using never-heard-of vocabulary words to describe missionary and theological theory. One of my favorites is the word *autochthonous*, a Greek word that combines the concepts of "self" and "soil." Literally translated this word means "people materialized from the earth by themselves." A bit more help comes from Merriam-Webster's dictionary, which defines the word as "formed or originating in the place where found." As it relates to church planting, this word describes something that wasn't imported but rather something truly "of the soil" in a given region.

Eugene Nida, a linguist and Bible translator, uses the word *autochtonous* to describe a church movement in Latin America with three qualifiers:

1. The churches developed spontaneously, without a history of missionary involvement,

2. The churches were planted by missionary efforts of other Latin American autochthonous churches, or

3. The churches were formerly mission-related but broke foreign links and reflect the people's culture in the deepest sense.

I would use similar qualifiers to describe the areas of tremendous church growth throughout South Asia. The churches we assist in India and Sri Lanka are genuinely homegrown congregations. They aren't being led by or funded by outsiders, and those who attend these churches aren't joining a "foreign religion." It is *theirs*. God has done work in their culture, and their churches have grown up as a result. The wider body of Christ has certainly served these congregations through the training of leaders, the contributions of startup funds for church planting, or even through encouraging visits from India Gospel League partners. But the owners of the churches are the people themselves.

These churches are uniquely "of the soil" in South Asia. As such, they are able to reach their own communities, train up new disciples, and multiply to surrounding villages much more effectively than outsiders ever could.

JUMPSTART

If a car battery is found dead on a cold morning, what it often needs is simply a "jumpstart," whereby power from a nearby car is used get the engine running. The only reason jumpstarting a car works is because once the power has been transferred, the cable can be disconnected and the revived motor can operate on its own.

This metaphor is something akin to what I see in the biblical model of church growth when new cultures were introduced to the gospel for the first time. Certainly cross-cultural missionaries such as Paul and Silas were critical in the founding of New Testament churches. Sometimes they would stay only a few days to plant gospel seeds (as in Athens), and at other times they would invest months or years in laying a solid foundation for a new congregation (as in Ephesus). But ultimately the "cables" were disconnected, and the church was directed by its own leaders, appointed from their own cultural group.

The book of Titus gives us an example. When Paul wrote to Titus, he told his protégé, "This is why I left you in Crete, so that you might put what remained into order, and appoint elders in every town as I directed you" (Titus 1:5). Paul's long-range vision was that the churches of Crete would be led by their own elders, and then the jumpstart of a Christian presence on the island would be complete.

I also see examples in how Peter was used by God to share the gospel with the household of Cornelius and how Philip shared Christ with the Ethiopian. Both of these jumpstarts were short term. The Lord himself was building the church, and He was using His witnesses to spread Good News.

> I THINK WE BEGIN MISSING KAIROS MOMENTS WHEN WE BEGIN "ORGANIZING" MOVEMENTS OF THE HOLY SPIRIT.

The point of Peter's and Philip's interactions was not to bring "Jerusalem-style church" into new places. The culture of the Ethiopians was quite different from the culture in Israel, and the customs common in Cornelius' family differed greatly from those found among the churches of Asia Minor. I do not believe God wanted all of these cultures to blend together somehow or to align themselves with the style of worship and practice of a central hub; rather, His intent was for those respective churches to relate the gospel into their own cultures, all for the furtherance of God's kingdom everywhere on earth.

We don't need to plant American churches in Sri Lanka for the same reason we probably don't need to plant a Sri Lankan church in Germany (unless, of course, it happens to be populated by Sri Lankans). Every culture needs a church of its own that speaks the language of its people and whose customs and worship can be born out of the Holy Spirit's work in that culture.

I think we begin missing *kairos* moment opportunities when we begin "organizing" the movement of the Holy Spirit. Churches are as unique as the people who attend them. The gospel, of course, is a fixed reality, as is any core doctrine in the Scriptures. But the expressions of style and strategy are best practiced when they are *autochthonous* rather than imported.

We must to resist the urge, as cultural outsiders, to define how things "should" happen based on our own experiences. Jesus Christ is the "only way," but our church style is not! To fulfill the Great Commission in this generation, then, we need to pray for and look for God to raise up "of the soil" laborers to go into His harvest fields. To that end, Jesus instructed us to pray: *"The harvest is plentiful, but the laborers are few. Therefore pray earnestly to the Lord of the harvest to send out laborers into his harvest"* (Luke 10:2).

I am comfortable trusting God with the strategy to build His church and to grow His eternal family. He asks me simply to obey. After all, as Paul reminded the Corinthians: *"So neither he who plants nor he who waters is anything, but only God who gives the growth"* (1 Cor. 3:7).

HOW MANY?

The cost of sending one U.S. based missionary family to South Asia, not including extensive seminary and linguistic training, approaches $100,000 per year, in addition to administrative and deputation expenses. Supporting a church planter in India Gospel League's network requires just $2400 for the two year "jumpstart" period before his ministry becomes self-sufficient.

FOR FURTHER DISCUSSION

1. Consider the ministry style of the church you attend. In what ways does it reflect cultural expectations and norms in your community?

2. Have you ever been involved in supporting or training indigenous Christian workers in another culture? Has your church? If so, what have the results been from these partnerships?

3. The need to grow churches "of the soil" in other nations is rather obvious. How might this concept apply to church planting in your own nation or among different cultural groups within your city? When should a church be intentionally "multi-cultural," and when should its approach be culture-specific?

CHAPTER 6

CROSSING CULTURES, CREATING VALUE

I realize that this line of reasoning sets up some tensions.

At this point, you might be asking yourself, "What can be said about so many mission efforts already in progress that seem outside of this indigenous paradigm? What about those in history that have had great success sharing the gospel in cultures beyond their own and even exporting denominational models of Christianity? What about families and friends who have felt called by the Lord to live and serve overseas?"

I would first of all say there is a place for cross-cultural mission efforts! Cultures do need one another, and those with the gospel must certainly be ready and willing to share it with those that have never heard. It is important for every believer to have a Great Commission mindset, and to take action to share the gospel as Jesus commanded. The New Testament teaches this clearly, and the early Christians modeled it well. How to do so is the question. Here is where I recommend beginning, by asking this question: "What does God want to do *through me?*"

Right at the outset, this is the critical question to answer.

Some people get caught up in their own dream for what they would like to do for God rather than really seeking what God would like to do through them. What if God is calling you to serve Him or to live out His call in a way different than what you want? Are you open to do whatever He calls you to do?

I imagine we will always battle against our preconceived ideas with what we want to do, what we are equipped for, and with what we've been taught in the past. As long as our own agendas and expectations can be laid down in deference to Christ's vision, I think we will be on the right road.

There was a time in the eighteenth century when pioneering mission efforts around the world were desperately needed and yet very few Christians had a mentality that said, "I will go!" During that time period, an Englishman named William Carey was called by God to go and jumpstart mission efforts in India, but he was told by his peers not to bother. One even said, "If God chooses to convert the heathen, he can do it without your help or mine!" Talk about a wet blanket on evangelistic fire!

Thankfully Carey went ahead with his long boat ride to India and eventually won many souls to Christ, began educational efforts for the poor, and personally translated the Bible into multiple Indian languages. God used Him mightily in the history of my people! But in order to seize that *kairos* moment, Carey had to push past the suspicions, prejudices, and denominational structures of his day. He had to launch out boldly and do what others had not thought of doing. And the fruit is obvious: many Christian churches in India had their genesis in Carey's faith and sacrifice for the gospel.

The needs of this hour are different, but the call of the gospel is the same. Just like William Carey, God may ask you to do what hasn't been done, what your peers can't yet understand, or something that will result in a dramatic rearrangement of "church-as-usual" Christianity. God may call you to seize a *kairos* moment in your city, nation, or somewhere else on the globe.

India Gospel League invites people from around the world to participate in what God is doing here through partnership with the local churches. How that invitation came to be is a story to tell in itself, which I will come to in the next chapter. For now, I'd like to address some principles of ministering cross-culturally that hopefully can be strategic in your endeavors to fulfill the Great Commission.

CROSS-CULTURAL PRINCIPLE #1 – ARE WE BEING HUMBLE?

It should go without saying that a defining characteristic of Christian life and witness is humility. In our fallen world, however, sometimes pride interrupts our missionary endeavors without our even realizing it. I'd like to present some questions you might ask any time you seek to minister to another cultural group, whether in your own country or beyond. Sending organizations and church mission teams can ask these questions of themselves as well when it comes to their interactions with foreign church leaders.

- Am I doing it for God or for me?

- Am I in the position of a servant to the local believers or an overseer?

- Am I perceived as a partner or a director?

- Am I advancing their goals or my own?

- Am I investing in their work or trying to gain influence over it?

- Am I going in as an encourager or as some sort of expert?

I only pose such difficult questions because I know the history of mission efforts. Sadly, many attempts to carry the gospel forward have failed due to pride, racism, misunderstanding, personal agendas, and organization building.

India Gospel League needs visionary believers from all across the world who will pour time, prayer, effort, money, and expertise into advancing the kingdom in places where Jesus has never been named, or where resources to grow and strengthen churches are scarce. But we also need those visionaries to be humble in their philosophy and wise about their approach, just as we must remain humble in ministering among the many people groups in our own region.

A servant-hearted, humble attitude is the most important part of effectively reaching other cultures for Christ. And He himself showed us the way, did He not? "Do nothing from selfish ambition or conceit, but in humility count others more significant than yourselves . . . Have this mind, which is yours in Christ Jesus, who, though he was in the form of God, did not count equality with God a thing to be grasped, but emptied himself, by taking the form of a servant" (Phil. 2:3-7).

CROSS-CULTURAL PRINCIPLE #2 – IS THE GOSPEL CENTRAL?

A trend in Christian mission efforts over the last few centuries has been to "lead with compassion" and then look for ancillary opportunities to share the gospel or to plant churches. I have come to question the effectiveness of that approach, which is why *India Gospel League leads with the gospel.*

I have no interest in critiquing the good works others have done, so I speak merely from my own organization's experience and convictions. The ministry of India Gospel League is based in one of the most impoverished, needy areas on the planet. According to one U.N. study (2014), India is home to one-third of the world's "extreme poor" – or, those subsisting on less than $1 a day. If ever there was a place that compassionate outreach was needed, it is here!

However, even in areas of great physical need, we must never lose sight of this reality: the deepest needs of the human condition are *spiritual*. People change from the inside out!

While making the gospel central, then, how do we help with the great needs we see? The sick? The orphaned? The poor? The illiterate? *Our strategy is to share the compassionate blessings of Christian love to people through local churches.* Every aspect of what we do and how we share humanitarian or educational help is designed to come from within a given community, based out of the local congregation of believers who can meet those needs wisely. New believers, even as they are receiving intensive Christian discipleship, are also offered skills-training for employment and community impact.

When the right time comes, assistance may even be given to a church to build a Life Center, which can become a resource to the whole community, in addition to becoming the meeting place for worship.

WHAT IF GOD IS CALLING YOU TO SERVE HIM OR LIVE OUT HIS CALL IN A WAY DIFFERENT THAN WHAT YOU WANT?

Prayerfully we assist community leaders in setting the patterns for community transformation, and in the long run, outside help becomes unnecessary. In this way, the ownership of community issues is local. *Villagers aren't taught to wait for foreign aid to stream in their direction; instead, they are equipped to serve one another.*

Remember Pastor Gideon and the "church on the dump"? That congregation has built homes for the people who once were living in that dump and then helped setup small cottage industries so that the population could lift itself out of such dire poverty.

Another story I like to share is one about a man named Daniel, who used to come to a leprosy feeding event where the gospel was presented. He was a most unusual candidate for becoming a church planter. His face was completely disfigured and his fingers ruined from leprosy. He heard the gospel at the feedings and became a Christian. Because he was living on the streets, we helped Daniel find a small house in which to live. He was so happy he began singing and praising the Lord, morning and evening. The neighbors became curious and wanted to know what could make this disfigured man so happy. He shared the gospel with them, and soon sixty people were gathering for prayer in his house. With our assistance, a church was established and a building was built.

Today, Daniel is still a church planter. He and his church are making a huge impact on their community. Some of his church members have initiated health and literacy programs. During the week, their Life Center is being used as a day care for children and a skills training center for women. In fact, these women have even started a production unit to manufacture garments, based right next to the Life Center.

Good works like these flow out of authentic churches as a matter of course, and that's why India Gospel League is committed to lead with the gospel first and then to empower the local believers to meet their own community needs. Without a church, it is difficult to imagine how disciples would be made, or how any practical assistance efforts could become self-sustaining.

Our ministry offers many ways for foreigners to partner with us to assist village churches in what they wish to provide for their community based on its needs. We can help them with economic development initiatives, literacy training, child sponsorship programs, medical clinics and more. The partnerships we set up are always *temporary*, designed so the local ministry efforts will become self-sustaining over the long-term. Rather than being perceived as "aid from the outside world," the help we provide is linked up with trustworthy pastors on the ground. Villagers understand that they are able to receive help from a church in their own neighborhood in partnership with a larger network of Christians.

Leading with the gospel is more than a strategic decision for us. It is a matter of conviction. The world needs Jesus and the change He brings into human hearts. In regions where idolatry and oppression have suppressed human creativity and dignity for generations (as in the still-prevalent caste system), more than money and food are needed. A transformation of life—new perspectives, family dynamics, forgiveness, self-worth, and new hope—can't be bought with aid dollars but is necessary for truly lifting those in need.

In contrast, I believe many mission groups, though well-intentioned, end up creating cyclical dependence on foreign aid and sadly, neglect to spread the gospel and plant churches. Foreign help without the gospel and the establishment of a local indigenously-led church relegates the help to a temporary uplift at best. At worst, it may create a sense of helpless entitlement among those being served.

CROSS-CULTURAL PRINCIPLE #3: ARE WE ADDING VALUE?

It is possible that people with good hearts can do good works that don't add up to real value in the lives of those being served. And while I believe that God honors good intentions, I think He honors good strategy all the more. If you are being presented with an opportunity to serve another culture, consider how you will be able to add real value to the kingdom in that context.

For example, one strategic decision we've made is that our network will not bring in outsiders to do direct evangelistic work. (Throughout South Asia, doing so would likely be detrimental to the work of local pastors in the long run due to a whole range of factors.) We do, however, invite friends from other lands in to help us train village pastors in theology, share medical expertise in our medical clinics, and take an "eyewitness trip" so that they can better understand what God is doing and then become a financial partner in one of India Gospel League's efforts. All of our short-term trips (many such trips occur every year) are designed to add specific value to the kingdom in a local context (see Appendix A for information on this).

I do not explain what India Gospel League does and how we do it to disparage other short-term (or even long-term) mission opportunities offered by churches and agencies whose efforts can provide much needed relief, assistance, and love. Instead, I want to challenge mission-minded Christians to evaluate carefully the way they can add maximum value to those they are reaching.

Rather than take for granted that our current methods are still effective and add value, let's seek God for His direction in any given mission endeavor, whether short or long-term, local or global. We want to be sensitive to obey the Holy Spirit as well as be generous, compassionate, loving, and strategic. How sad it is to think that during a *kairos* moment right now in world missions, some churches and organizations are being left out because they're operating on antiquated or insensitive paradigms.

Here are a few challenge questions you and I might ask as we consider mission opportunities. These questions could apply to a financial gift, a short-term trip, or a ministry project.

• What specific value am I seeking to add to people's lives?

• Have I researched any other ways to help add this kind of value?

• Am I certain that the approach taken will create long-lasting impact?

• What is motivating me to get involved?

• Is there a track record of this activity being fruitful?

• Do the costs of this opportunity align with the value being added?

Of course, answering these questions is a somewhat subjective exercise. But by asking them (and praying about them), we can help insure that our cross-cultural activities are useful to the kingdom. We should not only be interested in good intentions but good results! There is so much to accomplish for Christ, so many needs to meet, and so many fields ripe for harvest. We don't want to waste effort or energy or finances on something ineffective.

You might ask why we must take things so seriously, and evaluate results so rigorously? Paul explains his reasoning as an apostle: "This is how one should regard us, as servants of Christ and stewards of the mysteries of God. Moreover, it is required of stewards that they be found faithful" (1 Corinthians 4:1-2). In another place in Scripture, Paul famously explains that "we are ambassadors for Christ, God making his appeal through us" (2 Corinthians 5:20).

The gospel, and our responsibility to proclaim it to a world in great darkness, is a serious matter. The Lord holds us accountable not only for our intentions and attempts but also for the outcomes of our efforts (as in the Parable of the Servants, Matthew 25:14-30).

———————————

HOW MANY?

Children represent a dramatic ministry opportunity in South Asia today. In India alone, 400,000,000 children are age fourteen or younger. There are more children in India than there are people populating all of North America!

FOR FURTHER DISCUSSION

1. Have you traveled outside of your home country for mission purposes? What did you learn? What would you do differently if you went back?

2. How can you calculate the value you are adding when you or others you know travel on short-term mission trips? What factors could be considered?

3. How might you or your church balance its desire for short-term, cross-cultural trips with longer-term gospel partnerships?

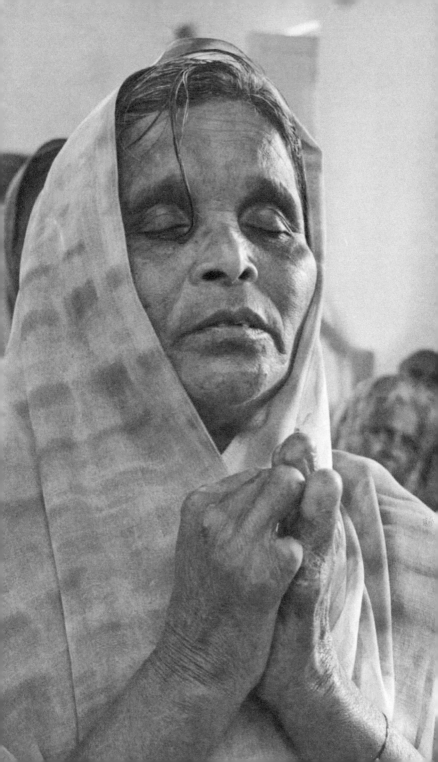

CHAPTER 7

PARTNERSHIP WITH GOD

W ould you like to engage in a partnership that would change lives?

"Put out into the deep and let down your nets for a catch," said Jesus. Simon, after an unsuccessful night of fishing in the very same waters, protested, but out of respect for this wise rabbi, went ahead and did as instructed. Suddenly, unexpectedly, a massive swell of fish began to overwhelm the nets!

Then the Lord invited Simon into a partnership that would change the world. "Don't be afraid, from now on you will catch men." And as Luke 5:11 records, Simon and his companions "brought their boats to land, they left everything and followed him."

What is striking about this invitation is how unnecessary Simon (later called Peter) actually was. Jesus didn't "need" Simon to catch men any more than He needed Simon to catch fish. But by His grace, the Lord invited him and a few other fishermen with him that day into a divine partnership, a worldwide fishing expedition for souls.

It would probably be appropriate to call the miraculous catch of fish in Peter's boat a sort of *kairos* moment. After all, the conditions were the same as the night before, from a human perspective. The lake was the same. The fish were the same. The skill of the fishermen involved and the quality of their tools were also the same. But something dramatic changed. Jesus got in the boat! For these rural fishermen, the ultimate "opportune time" popped up right in front of them!

Peter could have had any number of alternate responses, and each would have changed the story:

- "Lord, I'm just too tired. Could I drop you off in my brother's boat over there, and he can take you out on the lake?"

- "Lord, you don't really need me anyway. I'd prefer just to watch you do your work from the shoreline."

- "Lord, I've already tried letting down the nets and it didn't work. But I do have some other ideas on how we might be successful today."

- "Lord, my family has been fishing in this lake for generations. We know what we are doing, and we don't see any reason to change our methodology."

- "Lord, the fish in this lake aren't biting. But my brothers and I are thinking of heading into town for a hot breakfast. Would you like to join us?"

This story teaches us a few important things about *kairos* moments:

We can't create them. We can fish all night in our own strength and catch nothing. Peter could have applied the best of his training, the best of his strategy, the best of his intuition—and none of it would have led to this net-busting, boat-sinking school of easy-to-catch fish!

We can't explain them. When the power of Jesus starts working, our fishing methods are quickly overwhelmed. Peter didn't stroll into town and start mentioning how great a fisherman he was. It wasn't new netting or new methods. Something supernatural had occurred!

We aren't necessary! Jesus used Peter, Andrew, James, and John to participate in this *kairos* moment. But He could have used anyone else. He could have just done it on His own! In God's grace, He chooses to let people partner with Him in *kairos* moments, particularly those individuals with the faith to obey His directives.

GOD'S FELLOW WORKERS

From that point forward, Jesus began collecting disciples who in turn spread the message of His coming far and wide. At one point, recorded in Luke 10, he mobilized seventy-two disciples to go throughout Israel to prepare people to meet with Him. What all-powerful Jesus could have done with a snap of his fingers, He instead chose to do through willing-hearted followers.

The same is true today, for us. God invites us to participate in

His work (a far cry from us inviting God to participate in ours).

Paul wrote of this fact in 1 Corinthians 3:5-9, confronting the church for dividing itself on the basis of human leadership. "What then is Apollos? What is Paul? Servants through whom you believed, as the Lord assigned to each. I planted, Apollos watered, but God gave the growth. So neither he who plants nor he who waters is anything, but only God who gives the growth. He who plants and he who waters are one, and each will receive his wages according to his labor. For we are God's fellow workers. You are God's field, God's building."

Simply put, we are God's fellow workers. Whether in Hyderabad, Hanoi, or Houston, whether on a university campus or in a village children's home, we work with Him and for Him. We are partners with God, and He works through us. The more responsive we become to His presence and power in a situation, the more we can be a part of the opportune moments He creates for His kingdom's advance.

PARTNERSHIP AS A MINISTRY MODEL

It is natural when we form a partnership to think about benefits that flow both ways—that is, how we can structure the arrangement so value is distributed equally to the partners involved. When we fully understand that "neither he who plants nor he who waters is anything, but only God who gives the growth" (1 Cor. 3:7), then our framework for partnering with others changes radically.

But what of this idea that all of us are actually partners with God?

If we accept this idea, then for me to serve you doesn't necessitate some agreement wherein you would serve me back. We wouldn't be operating on those terms. Rather, we would seek to maximize glory to God and the advancement of His purposes, regardless of who benefits in an earthly sense.

Here is how some *kairos* moments have been missed. When individuals, organizations, or denominations mix in their own agenda for growth with the broad objective of growing God's kingdom, they can start to confuse the lines between partnership for God's glory and partnership for their own advancement. The history of Christianity across the world is littered with too many stories of broken relationships, wrong motivations, and needless divisions because the math of a given partnership was or became oriented horizontally (toward people) instead of vertically (toward God).

> *THE MORE RESPONSIVE WE BECOME TO HIM IN A SITUATION, THE MORE WE CAN BECOME PART OF THE OPPORTUNE MOMENTS THAT HE CREATES FOR HIS KINGDOM'S ADVANCE.*

Imagine the disciples Peter and Andrew being worried about the growth of their fishing organization during their *kairos* moment, when the fish started weighing down their nets. Rather than calling for help from a nearby boat (crewed by John and James), they might have tried to haul in the whole catch on their own, limiting the number to what their own systems could handle. Or even worse, after the catch, they might have begun calculating what this new business model would mean and neglected the larger call to become "fishers of men" altogether. After all, Peter might have been able to write a bestseller on one of the greatest fish stories ever told.

Any of those scenarios would have missed the point entirely. Jesus was (and is) the point! And His willingness for us to be "fellow laborers" in the harvest field has nothing to do with us, our organizations, our brands, our feelings, our claims, or even our measures of success. He has invited us to partner together for His glory!

In the early 1990s, I had to make a mental switch from thinking of "growing our organization" toward partnering with the men and women God was raising up around India to serve them so that they could reach Asia's unreached millions. It was work God was already doing, and with or without India Gospel League, He would still do it. We were and still are just among those fishing boats nearby the miracle. There are certainly others God is using too.

The biblical account of the miraculous catch of fish came up in the early days of India Gospel League's *kairos* moment that led to the church planting movement. In fact, I gleaned some application principles from that story to share as a four-part challenge to our frontline workers:

1. Go out into the deep waters. That "deep" may be the unreached areas where the gospel has never been heard.

2. Say "yes" to Christ in faith. Peter obeyed even when human logic told him that things didn't make sense.

3. Expect God's power in the situation. When the fishermen obeyed, the results were obvious and overwhelming.

4. Let God receive all the credit and glory.

When we encouraged church planters to launch into the deep with these principles, in short order they were catching far more than they could handle!

MORE BOATS

Every time I stand up in front of audiences in other parts of the world, particularly when speaking about mission efforts, I invite people to partner with us. But that invitation isn't about the growth of India Gospel League because the ministry in itself is really a partnership of thousands of church planters and workers in Asia. The partnership I talk about with audiences isn't a deal I'm trying to make. It's just an invitation to help us pull in the "Third Wave" miraculous catch of fish that Jesus is bringing forth in our region today. It's an invitation to help us put more nets in the water by bringing more boats to the scene of this modern-day miracle.

We can't handle the catch on our own. What God is doing is far bigger than our organization.

As an example, one of the core opportunities I present is our "barefoot pastor" sponsorship program. It is a simple, inexpensive way to help a church planter get started. Often these pastors are already trying to plant churches without any resources or formal training. Many of them are bi-vocational, meaning they have to work long hours to earn enough money to feed their families. India Gospel League helps these faithful servants find fellowship with other church planters and theological training, and we arrange sponsorship of their ministry for two years so that they can get one or two new congregations started. After two years, the pastor and his family are supported by the church(es) they have planted.

In addition to sponsorship, we also help the pastor seek the Lord for vision and strategy. We don't tell him what to do. We don't override his sense of calling with our own. Instead, we come alongside him in partnership, connecting him with needed resources and training.

As you can see from this example, the invitation I might give someone to "partner with India Gospel League" is really an invitation to partner with this particular pastor, his wife, and his children. From there, after the planting and watering, God is the one who makes the new church(es) grow.

Most of the pastors connected to India Gospel League and the Vision 2000 movement are generating their own bold strategies to reach cities, states, and nations. Many have started church-based pastoral training programs for their young people. Almost all of them have active evangelistic and children's outreach goals. They are starting compassionate care ministries for the leprous, the disabled, the poor, and the orphaned. These outreaches aren't a part of an imposed blueprint from another place. They are instead locally-grown ideas in the hearts of pastors and their church people who are seeking the Holy Spirit's direction to best lead their communities to Christ and then to expand the gospel into never-before reached areas around them.

Believe me when I say that tens of thousands of young church congregations in rural regions have certainly stretched our "nets." There are immense logistical challenges in trying to share training, encouragement, resources, and fellowship with this exponentially widening circle of affiliated Christian leaders. And yet God has been gracious to us, sending us the needed resources from people around the globe.

We do our best to keep track of the number of churches spawning off of the Vision 2000 network. Our reports indicate now that literally hundreds more are being added every month. The vast majority of these new congregations are already self-sustaining and require no financial support. Others, particularly in the least reached regions, need startup funding to get the evangelism and church planting efforts underway.

PARTNERSHIP MINISTRY—FOR YOU?

This partnership mentality about ministry has allowed us to engage extensively in India's *kairos* moment of church planting and make a significant impact, much more than if we were trying to do it on our own. It makes me wonder how many kingdom opportunities have been lost over the centuries because, rather than partnership, someone sought to exercise control, imposed a strategy from a different culture, or couldn't adjust to the changing realities of a dynamic situation. *How many people have missed a chance to do something bold with God because their organization or denomination wasn't the one leading the effort?*

On Judgment Day, we may discover what could have been, what areas of the world might have been reached, or even what special moments we could have been a part of if only we had laid down our pride and preconceived notions. And just as this thought is striking in a corporate sense (what if God's people through the centuries had served the kingdom more selflessly?), it is also true in a very personal sense. What might be different in my life today if I had always set self aside and thought of myself as a true partner with Jesus? Have I missed opportunities because I had tunnel vision into my own way of doing things or toward the growth of my organization? Have *kairos* moments already come and gone?

It is certainly a matter for prayer. I don't recommend that we get too carried away, however, with what might have been possible in the past. We can look back, learn the lessons, and prepare to carry on. There is still a world to reach, there is still light to shine, and there are still limitless opportunities to serve and share with the least and the lost.

What if we prayed something like this?

> "Lord, I want to be sensitive to Your kairos moments, the opportune times when You empower people

and arrange situations to grow Your kingdom and establish Your name. If I have fallen prey to a me-first mentality or even a my-church-first mentality, I repent of it. I am just one of millions who are called to serve You. It doesn't matter if I get 'credit' in the eyes of my fellow servants. It doesn't matter if the people I reach think of 'Paul' or 'Apollos' (or me) as their leader. You are the one who makes things grow, and I count it a privilege to play any part in the process. My whole life is for You, Jesus!"

_____

HOW MANY?

One out of seven people on earth lives among India's unreached people groups.

FOR FURTHER DISCUSSION

1. How might you determine the difference between me-first ministry and the kind of ministry that seeks God's kingdom first?

2. Why is it important to encourage permanent self-sufficiency among new churches and their pastors? In your view, is this merely a good idea, or is it a critical one?

3. When was the last time you acted as a "partner with God" in accomplishing His kingdom work?

CHAPTER 8

IT IS TIME

Now is the opportune time. We need to see the world with a kingdom perspective. I'm speaking of God's vision for every culture, tongue and tribe in my country and around the world.

God's vision for India is simply an extension of His global, kingdom vision. Perhaps every person in India will not become a believing Christian, but I can imagine a day when the majority of Indian citizens are worshiping the living God, Jesus Christ, and the values of His kingdom—justice, equality, and peace—are planted deeply in the cultural context of the nation.

Imagine it happening in your nation! What stands in the way of it coming to pass? I came across a great slogan that might apply: "The best way to church the unchurched might be to unchurch the churched!" I'm sure that's not the entire answer, but it is certainly part of it.

In some places, churches have grown so formal and institutional that they have lost their vitality as part of a people movement that can continue to grow by itself. In some

> KAIROS *MOMENTS WILL SURFACE AS THE SAVIOR TAKES YOUR MEAGER LOAVES AND FISHES AND MIRACULOUSLY FEEDS THE MULTITUDES.*

cases, the growth itself took away the health of the church because people became too dependent on the institution (this may even be true of some "modern churches" I have encountered). The incarnational presence of God in our churches needs to be felt in our communities. It's not just a matter of style or prose. Some structures need to be broken down and re-thought entirely.

The church was always meant to be a *vibrant people movement.*

To me this is a major principle that needs to be recovered. The central mission of the church is not about polity, budget allocations, staff benefits, or building programs. It isn't about "making churchgoers" or even "making believers." Jesus wants us to go and *make disciples*!

If the institutionalized, professionalized church of modern times is in fact part of what needs to change, how will these changes begin? If the very structures we've come to depend on are what hinder us from seeing and responding to *kairos* moments, where do we start? Part of the answer is for each of us to take the situation to the Lord in prayer, and part of it, I submit, is in the hands of church leaders.

India Gospel League has been laying great emphasis on this principle among the young churches of South Asia, prayer-fully, so they recognize that *multiplication* is a higher value to the kingdom than some specific form of organization. We teach every church planter that after a church is planted, the pastor and other disciples of that church are to multiply by going out and planting more churches.

Ephesians 4:11-13 explains God's strategy: "And he gave the apostles, the prophets, the evangelists, the shepherds and teachers, to equip the saints for the work of ministry, for building up the body of Christ, until we all attain to the unity of the faith and of the knowledge of the Son of God, to mature manhood, to the measure of the stature of the full-ness of Christ."

Churches, led by biblical leaders, should be at the forefront of changing everything around them rather than letting the culture change them. If you are a church leader today, God has put a small portion of His flock under your care, and it is your responsibility to discern the times in which your church lives. What is God doing? How is He calling your church to participate? What will the strategy be to stay engaged and to take the next steps in building the kingdom?

A great challenge for us in India right now is to avoid setting in motion the kind of systems that would perpetrate the very error I am trying to address in this book. We have to be careful not to grow a new kind of structure that would ren-der future leaders in our nation unable to discern the *kairos* moments of their generation. We are teaching and training our people not to get too structured, to always empower new believers for evangelism, and to keep the Great Commission in sharp focus. And we are trying to keep the ownership of the church's mission *personal*. Every individual believer must understand his and her part in the growth and health of the church. People must not think that "leadership will take care of this." Such thinking would be the beginning of the end of our kingdom impact.

Recently the India Gospel League leadership team gathered to celebrate a special milestone in our organizational history, and we shared some rich times of fellowship and prayer. We celebrated the fact that God has been using thousands of faithful Christian workers to do His will—pastors as well as schoolteachers, regional trainers, women's study leaders, youth leaders, Children's Gospel Club directors, medical personnel, house parents at children's homes—the list is long! We committed ourselves as an 'extended family' to strive always in the years ahead to:

- live out the incarnational presence of Jesus through everything that we do rather than become a huge institution.

- remain focused on effectiveness rather than growth.

- measure success not with how much we have gathered but on how much we have "scattered" for the kingdom.

- make sure our lives speak louder than our words.

My earnest prayer is that we can continue to see the movement of God's Spirit touching lives and transforming communities across South Asia, where so many people are in so much need, and where so many have never heard the gospel. And my prayer is also for you, that in your nation and in your context, you also can see "book of Acts" activity for God's honor and the expansion of His kingdom.

NOT JUST FOR INDIA

After reading about the *kairos* moment in India in this book, you might be tempted to say, "Well, even so, this particular move of God is in Asia and not here, wherever I live."

Let me encourage you: all who actively engage in the Great Commission and put these principles to work will see how and where God is working. They will see the transformation that only He can bring. *Kairos* moments will surface as the Savior takes your meager loaves and fishes and miraculously feeds multitudes. Streams of living water will appear in the desert before you.

Applying these principles in India doesn't mean that every village will respond to the gospel, nor does it mean that rough ground will be plowed without hard, sacrificial work. But it does mean that when Jesus tells us where to cast our nets, everything can change in a heartbeat.

I began this book with two premises:

1. **A *kairos* moment is occurring in South Asia today.** It is worthy of attention and support. I gladly ask you to

consider partnering with India Gospel League to help us continue jumpstarting new churches in new regions and then equipping those churches to serve their communities, then to multiply to neighboring communities. We must finish the task our Savior entrusted to us, to "preach the gospel to all creation" (Mark 16:15). Thousands of villages still need their first gospel witness, and in them, millions of people need to experience the love and blessing of a relationship with Jesus.

2. **A *kairos* moment can occur in your life today.** Are you ready to see what God is doing, to listen for God's direction, and to join Him? Sometimes the answer will involve letting go of traditions or well-worn excuses, and it might even mean changing your Great Commission paradigms altogether. With faith in God's power and prompt obedience to His voice, any empty fishing boat can suddenly be filled. Any place of darkness can be flooded with light. Any desert can be flooded with living water.

God has worked in powerful ways since the beginning. Today is no different! If we turn back to the basics—seeking and obeying the Holy Spirit, responding obediently to God's call—we will see His work flourish. The principles I have outlined in this book work every time they are tried. They are not my ideas. They are right out of God's Word.

My friend, the opportune time is now. Don't let another *kairos* moment pass without responding. Urgently pray, and then boldly obey.

———————————————

HOW MANY?

God is entrusting you with 1,440 minutes today to honor Him and to advance His kingdom. Which of these moments are opportune for kingdom impact?

FOR FURTHER DISCUSSION

1. How has this book modified your expectations of how God accomplishes His work?

2. Be they in India or elsewhere, are you prepared to forge stronger global partnerships to reach areas that have never heard the gospel?

3. What would change about your day if you treated it as a *kairos* moment?

A FINAL WORD

This book has emphasized what God has done, and to an even greater extent, what He is still doing. In this final word, I'd like to turn your attention to the *future* – not only the future of India Gospel League, but of the Christian movement across the world.

There is so much work yet-to-be-done for the glory of God across the planet. Millions of people wander without the light of the gospel. Nations struggle against one another, persecution against religious minorities is prevalent in many places. At the same time, mission movements are spreading into areas that have been in darkness for centuries and modern technology is making it possible to communicate the gospel further and faster than ever before. Just as paradigms have shifted in the past, we expect them to continue to shift – for better, and for worse (in an earthly sense).

Will we accomplish the mission Jesus entrusted to us, in this generation? Will the next generation hear the gospel? Will nations like mine finally have the light of Jesus shining in every city, in every village? How about in your nation? Will the whole world see the love of Christ flowing out from His church?

And as God orchestrates *kairos* moments, will we be responsive to His Spirit?

India Gospel League is focusing attention on four critical priorities, which we believe are key to the effectiveness of 21st century believers in our culture. I offer them here to serve as a concluding encouragement to you, as you walk forward in your own life and ministry.

1. Discipleship & Christian Education. At the core of the Great Commission (Matthew 28:19-20) is, of course, discipleship – after baptizing new believers, we must "teach them to obey" all that Christ commanded.

Since the first century, this has been the linchpin issue of the expansion of God's kingdom on earth. While I believe we must set specific and aggressive goals to reach neighborhoods and nations with the gospel message, we also must take the same intentional approach at carrying through with the rest of the discipleship process (Colossians 2:6). Discipleship is a *lifelong process* of learning about God, self, family, the church, society, the world and how all these things connect to God's purposes for human life. Emphasizing this priority, and being meticulous about its implementation, can help ensure the emergence of a strong and healthy church that will be vibrant in its faith, contextual in its witness, equipped to multiply, fully sustained and empowered to transform. Perhaps this intentionality is what Paul was describing in Colossians 1:28-29, when he said, "[Christ] we proclaim, warning everyone and teaching everyone with all wisdom, that we may present everyone mature in Christ. For this

I toil, struggling with all his energy that he powerfully works within me."

In India, we seek to empower everyday believers to become bold witnesses, and as people come to Jesus, we want to be sure the church is ready to give them the training, love, and attention they need to "grow in the grace and knowledge of our Lord Jesus Christ" (2 Peter 3:18). We believe it is critical that every believer is firmly grounded in his or her faith, through a deep knowledge and understanding of God's Word. Of course, the aim is that they be truly equipped to apply this in their daily lives, which is why systematic and robust Christian education is so important to us.

We have also decided to lay strong emphasis on the discipleship of children and young people, through our "Children's Gospel Clubs" and "Y21" movement. Hundreds of thousands of youth have been trained not only to share their faith, but to walk with God on a daily basis. We aim to make this an even greater point of focus in the years ahead!

2. Leadership Development. Bill Hybels once wrote that, "The local church is the hope of the world, and its future rests primarily in the hands of its leaders." In my culture, particularly in the rural areas, most believers are first or second generation. That means we are in great need of character-qualified, servant-hearted, biblically-rooted, Christ-focused leaders, just like the churches of the first century were in need of such individuals.

Many pastors here are new believers themselves, opening God's Word weekly and doing the best they can with minimal training. That puts a premium on whatever leadership or theological training can be offered. I see this as among the most strategic investments we can make in the future of the South Asian church.

We spend a large proportion of our efforts pouring into the lives of tomorrow's leaders, believing that these seeds will grow into a mighty harvest of kingdom activity. In fact, we've already seen the fruit of this approach – some of our early Children's Gospel Club participants are now church planting pastors, and many of our church planters have become regional leaders and trainers of many others. This dynamic showcases the vision that Paul outlined in 2 Timothy 2:2, where disciples begin making other disciples, and where leaders entrust God's Word to future leaders.

3. Community Impact. Another component of strategic vision that we have been emphasizing in India is the need for churches to take an active role in specific community engagement. We've encouraged the churches to work intentionally at serving their communities – to become centers of early childhood education and adult skills training, launching points for medical clinics and economic development initiatives, and to care for those most in need.

Of course, the needs of every village are unique, and whatever initiatives are taken are selected by the local believers. Rather than prescribing precisely what any congregation should do to reach out, our trainings and programs are designed to equip pastors and their people to have an outward-facing mentality about the world around them, to be the "hands and feet" of Jesus in the village.

4. Multiplication. To finish the global task of sharing the gospel, we must think beyond growing individual churches or organizations. Rather, we must emphasize multiplication – believers multiplying themselves through evangelism and discipleship; congregations multiplying themselves through leadership development and church planting.

One way we're working to add this into the culture of the South Asian church is to help believers develop a *multiplication mentality.* Every believer is encouraged to take training in evangelism so he or she can share the gospel, and every church planted is encouraged to pray about where the next church may be needed in their given region. The growing network of Vision 2000 church planters have each prayerfully committed to start one new church every year, by God's grace. In recent times, this commitment has borne significant fruit – hundreds of new churches are starting every month!

WHERE DO WE GO FROM HERE?

At a recent gathering of the entire India Gospel League leadership team, along with many pastors and friends, I shared these four priorities along with our specific action plans to increase focus on these areas. More than any other objective we could set, the one I believe would most transform our culture is *that every village would have a church dedicated to these four priorities.* And so, by God's grace, that is our goal – that every one of India's 650,000 village communities would have a church.

I don't share these four priorities to say that somehow we've stumbled onto a new formula for church growth – on the contrary, I see these as some of the most basic biblical principles we see modeled in the book of Acts. At every turn, we've discovered that the more churches humbly, prayerfully focus on these priorities, the more kingdom fruit they bear.

Let's keep our eyes on the harvest, my friends, to see what must be done, and what amazing opportunities await. And let us also keep our eyes on Christ, the author of every *kairos* moment, in my nation, or in yours.

For His glory,

Sam Stephens

APPENDICES

APPENDIX A

COME AND SEE!

Would you like to be an eyewitness to the *kairos* moment in South Asia today?

India Gospel League can put you on the front lines of the gospel advance and even provide you with opportunities to engage directly with believers in rural villages. Our team at the North American office can help you plan a trip that fits your family, church, or corporate budget as well as works with your schedule and matches your passions to make an eternal difference.

We help with the visa application process, coordinate your in-country accommodations on the Salem campus of our headquarters, and provide indigenous translators and trained guides for the duration of your trip.

Medical and Veterinary Teams: Medical teams that visit us will help conduct village medical camps according to the need and the practice areas of the visiting professionals. Some villagers served may not have seen a doctor in years or ever, so the relief for patients and joy for caregivers is immense. Previous teams have participated in dental clinics, eye care clinics, general medicine camps, gynecological seminars, veterinary camps, and many other specialties.

Eyewitness Teams: Eyewitness teams travel to India Gospel League headquarters in Salem, Tamil Nadu, to experience the breadth and depth of the ministry. Members may take part in leprosy feedings, church and home dedications, baptisms of new believers, micro-credit loan distributions, children's home visits, or distribution events for livestock and Bibles or many other helps available to be provided. Eyewitness trips are easily tailored to the passions of team members and can happen any time throughout the year.

Pastor, Women or Youth Teaching Teams: Teaching teams are an integral part of India Gospel League's ministry as we seek to train and empower our brothers and sisters in India to reach their nation for Christ. Team members travel the broad expanse of the country teaching at regional gatherings of pastors, women, and youth. Pastors, teachers, and Bible study leaders are welcome to join a teaching team.

Call 888.352.4451 or visit www.IGLWorld.org/Go for more information.

APPENDIX B

FIRST STEPS OF INVOLVEMENT

Would you like to partner with India Gospel League? We'd love to add you to the team! Christians from all across the world give time, energy, and financial resources to support the work of Christ in India and Sri Lanka. Here's how you can jump in:

1. **Begin praying for South Asia.** You might consider obtaining a map of India and becoming familiar with its states, people groups, and geography. Articles on specific needs, cultural challenges, and news updates are posted at www.IGLWorld.org. If you'd like to pray, consider the book *Operation World* by Patrick Johnstone. A wealth of information regarding the unreached people groups in India is available at www.JoshuaProject.net.

2. **Signup for resources.** When you visit the India Gospel League Web site, be sure to request your name to be added to the newsletter and email lists. You'll be kept in the loop on new developments from India and exciting ways to get involved personally. Link up with us on social media to get up-to-the-minute updates and also to share our projects with friends.

3. **Start a sponsorship.** You can support a barefoot pastor for monthly for a two-year commitment (or a one-time contribution). You'll receive a picture of the pastor and his family along with information about the ministry your sponsorship is making possible. On a quarterly basis, India Gospel League will send you updates on new villages being reached, testimonies from your pastor's ministry, and

personal prayer requests. You may also choose to sponsor needy children, adopt whole villages for transformation, and if you're interested in large-scale projects, adopt an entire unreached region involving hundreds of pastors. **To begin, visit www.IGLWorld.org or call the North American office at 888.352.4451.** (By the way, all contributions are tax-deductible and processed via the North American office in Hudson, Ohio.)

4. **Order extra copies of this book.** Help spread the challenge by sharing this book with friends and church leaders. Using the discussion questions, you could lead a small group or reading club through this material. Also, don't forget to order a copy of our book of encouraging stories about barefoot pastors, *Commissioned: How God is Changing Lives, Transforming Nations, and Involving You.*

5. **Get your kids engaged in a mission project.** Our Children's Gospel Clubs reach many thousands of South Asian children annually. The low cost of engagement makes this outreach a great partnership option for kids, Sunday school classes, and youth groups in other nations, who can sponsor the supplies needed for more kids to be discipled in the villages. It is a great way to give young hearts a global, Great Commission vision!

To give you an even better picture of the scope and depth of India Gospel League ministry, videos and audio interviews are posted on the Web site (www.IGLWorld.org) so you can get to know the team, see and hear stories of God's power, see projects we are working on, and grow your vision for what God is doing.

APPENDIX C

7 DAYS OF PRAYER FOR SOUTH ASIA

Would you pray for South Asia for a week? Feel free to copy and share this list as you wish.

☐ **DAY 1:** Pray for God to raise up additional laborers for this vast harvest field. Nearly one billion Indians live among unreached people groups. Even among those groups that do have the gospel, much work remains to be done.

☐ **DAY 2:** Pray for India Gospel League's barefoot pastors as they jumpstart churches among villages that have no Christian presence. Pray specifically for their perseverance, safety, and families as they proceed into sometimes-hostile and usually-difficult situations.

☐ **DAY 3:** Pray for the unity and blessing of the Lord on the nations in this region. Political and religious tensions exist, many tracing roots back to conflicts generations ago. Pray for peace and increased freedom for the area's population, particularly for minority groups that sometimes face persecution.

☐ **DAY 4:** Pray for the more than two hundred regions India Gospel League has identified in India that still need church-planting gospel movements to begin among them. Ask God to raise up laborers who can go into these areas and for the startup funding necessary.

☐ **DAY 5:** Pray for the 350,000+ villages that still need their first church plant. Ask God to embolden and empower the pastors to continue training additional leaders and intentionally multiplying churches as fast as possible.

☐ **DAY 6:** Pray for Sam and Prati Stephens, Pastor Benny, and the rest of the India Gospel League leadership team in Tamil Nadu. Specifically ask for God to give them wisdom to see the right next steps for the ministry and how to best encourage the thousands of Christian leaders who look to them for counsel.

☐ **DAY 7:** Pray for India Gospel League's children's ministries, medical outreaches, and economic development programs throughout South Asia. As a holistic ministry, we give attention not only on the spiritual aspects of life, but also the physical and emotional.

JOIN 10,000 IN PRAYER

We are building a list of 10,000 prayer warriors from across the world that are committed to lifting up our ministry in prayer regularly. If you'd like to join and receive bi-weekly emails with up-to-date prayer concerns, visit www.IGLWorld.org/Pray.

APPENDIX D

PRINCIPLES FOR EFFECTIVE MISSION PARTNERSHIPS

We are often asked about how individuals or churches can find the most effective mission partnerships. With so many agencies vying for attention (and for financial resources), it can be hard to distinguish what to do on two fronts:

- On a tactical level, which projects will be most effective?

- On a spiritual level, what is God calling you/your church to do?

Whether you are looking to advance the kingdom in Africa, Latin America, Asia, or anywhere else, you will want to hear positive answers to each of these before beginning a partnership:

1. **Is this project, idea, or agency centered on the Scriptures?** In every sense, genuine spiritual movements worthy of support find their bedrock foundations in the Bible. This trait should not be difficult to identify!

2. **Does it lead with the gospel?** We are always interested to see if a given strategy aims to attract people through compassionate works or if compassionate works flow out of lives changed by the gospel in local communities. India Gospel League has found the second approach to result in longer-lasting impact.

3. **Is it indigenously led?** We are very interested in "third wave" mission activity, that which is led and directed by

native believers, because the Holy Spirit is working powerfully through this wave in most regions of the world today. To see the Great Commission task advanced in our generation, we believe most mission partnerships should be third wave in nature.

4. **Is it designed to be self-sustaining?** A value we maintain is never to create dependency or an entitlement mentality among the people we are serving or partnering with. As such, our supported projects are temporary in nature and designed to use outside resources for startup (an exception to this rule may be found in some of our children's ministry work). For example, our sponsored pastors only receive two years of outside income before their new churches are expected to step in and support them going forward.

5. **Is it holistic?** I like to ask this question because I see in the ministry heartbeat of Jesus attention was given to all aspects of people's lives. Physical, emotional, and spiritual needs were met when Jesus came into a village. To the best of our ability, we aim to follow His example. Thus, we provide significant equipping and resourcing to local believers through which they can reach out to their communities with compassionate love, orphan care, medical treatment, and economic development. In this way, the local church becomes a hub of blessing and help to communities in great need.

INDIA GOSPEL *league*

1521 Georgetown Road, Suite 305

Hudson, Ohio 44236

888.352.4451

www.IGLWorld.org

Contact IGL to receive updates, join the prayer team, sponsor a pastor, support a project, or for information about traveling to India.

ABOUT THE AUTHOR

Samuel D. Stephens is the third generation leader of the India Gospel League, which was founded in the Salem District of Tamil Nadu in 1948 by Samuel's grandfather, Rev. Devaprasad Stephens. Sam served as a barefoot pastor until his father's death in 1988, when he assumed leadership of the ministry.

Sam's commitment to the advancement of the gospel, coupled with his desire to see sustainable transformation in poverty-stricken areas, has led him to be involved in work ranging from church planting to micro-credit lending initiatives, from the construction of a children's hospital to the building of schools and skills-training centers throughout South Asia. He is also founder of *The Sharon Cancer Center and General Hospital*, the *Non-Denominational Association of Interdependent Churches,* and the *Association of Indigenous Ministries.*

He and his wife Prati have nine children (seven of them adopted), and live with an "extended family" of more than 400 children, youth and adults at the beautiful Sharon ministry campus in Tamil Nadu, India.